# Meant For More

Igniting Your Purpose in a World That Tries to Dim Your Light

Charity Majors

ARISE

Arise Publishing House

Copyright © 2018 by Charity Majors

CharityMajors.com

All rights reserved.

No portion of this book may be reproduced, stored in a retrieval system, or transmitted in any form or by any means – for example, electronic, photocopy, recording – in any form without written permission from the publisher or author, except as permitted by U.S. copyright law. The only exception is brief quotations in printed reviews.

# Contents

| | |
|---|---|
| Grab your FREE Gift! | 1 |
| Dedication | 3 |
| Acknowledgments | 5 |
| Foreword | 7 |
| Introduction | 11 |
| This book is not what you think... | |
| Agreements | 16 |
| (Place your hand on your heart as you read the following): | |
| 1. Ready or Not...Here We Glow... | 19 |
| 2. What's Really Behind That Beautiful Selfie | 33 |
| 3. When Life Isn't All Rainbows & Glitter | 52 |
| 4. Put on Your Mud Boots | 67 |
| 5. Package That Matches the Contents | 89 |
| 6. Monkey Bars vs. Selfie Sticks | 97 |
| 7. Sticks and Stones | 108 |
| 8. Gift Bags for Everyone | 119 |
| 9. Bring on the Arrows | 137 |
| 10. Why, Yes, I'll Have Another... | 153 |

| 11. | A Magic Wand Life | 163 |
| --- | --- | --- |
| 12. | PS - One last thing before you go... Always remember: | 174 |
| References | | 175 |
| About the Author | | 176 |

# Grab your FREE Gift!

Get access to my FREE companion course (Retails for $97...yours FREE)!

Are you ready to unlock the potential inside of you so that you can make a meaningful impact on those around you? I have no doubt! You are #MeantForMore!

Get a head start by getting access to the online companion course, right now, by going to:

**CharityMajors.com/MeantForMore**

Simply enter in your email, which will create your username and password, and you can have instant access to the dozens of resources as you read through this book!

# Dedication

To the lover of my soul, the one that has formed me, fashioned me, and is so intimately close that He knows the numbers of hairs on my head. He knows my flaws, my mess ups, my hang ups, the good and the bad, and He still extravagantly loves me. The one who has called me, for such a time as this. My Source and Spirit. Jesus Christ. Thank you.

*To the amazing souls I get to share this life with: the ones that draw out the best in me, keep me grounded, make me laugh every day, and keep me on my toes.*

*My husband, Chris:* Thank you for always believing in me and encouraging me to go for it - whatever "it" may be. Next to every strong woman is an equally as strong counterpart, and I am grateful that you and your strength are beside me. I love you more today than ever, and there is no one else in the world I would rather adventure through this life with.

*My son, Judah:* You are my buddy, my partner, and my little love. You are so special to me, and you are one of the only ones who has listened to my heart from the inside. You are the reason I want to be who God called me to be...so I can be an example to you, because I believe you can change the world.

*To my daughter, our sweet baby girl, who was only meant for heaven:* I can't wait to hold you in my arms. Thank you for sharing your sweet spirit with me, if only for a short while. You have changed me in more ways than I will ever know.

*You three are my world, and I love you endlessly.*

To my parents, who gave me the loving foundation of who I am now believing I am, who always saw the best in me, and have been my biggest fans. I hope to be the type of parent that you have been to me. Thank you for living out a beautiful example of God's unconditional love, grace, and favor.

To my future self, the one who draws me to pursue the dreams she has already accomplished, the one who has journeyed through the fear I now face, and the one who gives me glimpses of what it's like - the lives that will be touched, the difference that will be made, and how fierce the fire is within me. Thank you. I will see you soon.

And to every one of you, who, like me, has felt like they were never enough or sometimes "too much," I see you. I feel you. I have been in your shoes and sometimes still wear them. We've got work to do. We can do this. We must do this, because our light, soul, and purpose is here for such a time as this.

# Acknowledgments

*To every beautiful soul (including my own inner voice) who told me I "couldn't do it" or "I should give up" or who told me "I didn't belong," or that "I didn't have what it took."*

Thank you. From the bottom of my heart, **thank you.** There is nothing but love, gratitude and compassion coming from my heart to yours. It's because of your words, that I received the lessons and the strength that I have to share these stories of hope and healing, in hopes that others may find healing in their own lives. Maybe one day, if you read this book, you will see how much you have impacted me for the better, so that I could go and make a difference in the world and help make it a brighter place. Maybe this book can do the same for you and one day, we will find that we are shining brightly together.

*To my Women Ignite and Unstoppable Influence, Bliss and Meant for More Tribes:*

Your love, friendship, encouragement, business knowledge and strategies, and the fact that we get to be on mission, together, is how I always dreamed it could be. You are the walking, living, breathing realization of those dreams and that we can have a world where women champion other women in the most beautiful way. From this grateful heart, thank you.

*To my photographer, Alex Garza:*

Thank you for being an integral piece to this beautiful cover puzzle. The way you see the world is beautiful.

*To my MaxGiving family:*

Thank you for believing in me, my message, and for showing it through your actions. Words could never express my gratitude, and I have no doubt this is just the beginning of what's to come.

# Foreword

**Foreword by Natasha Hazlett**

Charity Majors is the kind of person that lights up a room when she walks in. I was immediately drawn to her big smile and sunny disposition. I was surprised to learn that her positivity was something that was a source of ridicule for her growing up.

Some people think that being consistently "positive" is naïve or unrealistic. The reality is that being "positive" in the face of adversity is a skill. It's anything but naïve... A smile is a window to the soul, and the light that burns brightly within each and every one of us.

As I got to know Charity, I discovered that behind her glowing smile and positivity is a fierce commitment to personal and spiritual growth. She recognizes the light within her and has a desire to allow her own light to shine brightly in order to illuminate the path for others.

A passion to serve led Charity to immerse herself in the study of mentors and tools that equipped her to live a very purpose-driven life. The tools and strategies she gathered over the years have enabled her to take painful experiences and use them as lessons to help others.

In the age of picture-perfect selfies, it's not easy to pull off the mask, be vulnerable, and share the "real" story. But Charity Majors does just that in this impactful book.

Like Charity, I believe that we are all meant for more. And in this book, Charity guides readers through the journey to find what "more" could mean for them. *Meant for More* is filled with inspirational quotes and useful resources that will equip every reader for the road ahead.

Finding your purpose is a journey, not a destination. This book is the perfect step to get you started on the path to unlocking your purpose and making a meaningful impact in the world.

-*Natasha Hazlett*

Best-Selling Author, *Unstoppable Influence: Be You. Be Fearless. Transform Lives.*

## Foreword by Ronda Conger

I have had the honor to speak to the Mrs. Idaho contestants over the years, and I love to scan the crowd and try to pick the winner. I am looking for that contestant that has the best energy, the one that shines from the inside out. This is when I first met Charity Majors. She was different. She radiated beauty on so many levels. Yes, she was beautiful, but so much more. She was beautiful from the inside out - from her smile, from her passion, from her love for everyone she meets. Over the years, I have loved watching her shine and constantly work on all things in her life to share it with as many people as she can. She inspires me.

Charity's *Meant for More* is impactful, powerful, and something we all crave. We need to work on the full person, and Charity shows us the way! We all struggle with something... People are messy. Is it your self-confidence, which in turn hurts your exterior beauty? Or is that you are only focused on external beauty and you need a gut check?

If the answer is yes, this book is for you. Keep reading and get ready to shine. Charity has that effect on people!

*Meant for More* is right in line with my first book, *Better Human: It's a Full Time Job*. We are all far from done and need to work for it by reading, growing, and pushing ourselves. We all want to win. We all want to shine and become the best version of ourselves.

We've got work to do.

Let's go,

*-Ronda Conger*

National Speaker and Award-Winning Author of *Better Human*, *Better Thinking,* and *You Go First*

# Introduction
## This book is not what you think...

> "Everybody has a calling. And your real job in life is to figure out as soon as possible what that is, who you were meant to be, and to begin to honor that in the best way possible for yourself."
>
> -Oprah Winfrey
>
> #WeAreMeantForMore
> @CharityMajors

## This book is not what you think...

### How to get ready...

You won't find any perfect humans, perfect stories, perfect Instagram filters or perfect Pinterest pages within this book, so relax, let your guard down, you can be your totally awesome and imperfect self, too.

Hi, I'm Charity, and just like you, I am flawed. I mess up. I don't get it right. I wing it sometimes. I three-putt in golf. I get toilet paper stuck on my shoes. I fart. I change poopy diapers. I yell at the TV when my favorite sports team loses. I get stuck in my head. I sometimes let my fears hold me back. I feel like I'm not enough. I feel like I'm too much. There are days I don't shower. I can't keep a house plant alive to save my life. As a mom, I constantly feel like I am failing. I can't cook. I hate laundry. I compare myself to others. I take 20 different selfies and never post them because I don't like the way I look. I spend too much time on social media. I fumble. I go in circles. I hurt others. And even worse, I hurt myself.

#dontjudge
#youdoittoo
#letsbefriendsanyways
#perfectlyimperfecttogether

Now that we got that out in the open, I'm a firm believer that all of it—the ups and downs, the good and the bad, the beautiful and the ugly, the unraveling and the putting the pieces back together, the fears and the faith and "all the feels"—it is all a part of this beautiful human experience we came here to be a part of...and my friend, we are smack dab in the middle of it. There are some things that I have found, that helped get me out of the funk I sometimes find myself in, and it is my intention to share some within this book, but also provide even more outside of this book.

This book is meant to be more than words on a page or sharing of one's journey and stories of tragedy to triumph.

Because let's face it...stories are amazing and offer hope, but how many times have we heard or read a story only to leave wondering how the heck they went from point A to point C?! What was the stuff in the middle?! What was the "B?!" What were the resources that worked or the tool they used or the songs they danced to?! What was it that actually got them *out* of the wall-kicking moment besides just another affirmation?! (Because, by God, there are only so many affirmations you can tell yourself before something else has to be done!)

#beenthere

So, like I said, this book is meant to be an experience and a resource that not only offers you, the reader, inspiration and hope, but also the *actual tools* to implement in your life so that you can uncover more of who you are being called to be, get into action, shine brighter and pass that light onto others.

Within these pages you will find inspirational quotes that are meant to be a "pay it forward." If a quote resonates with you, take a photo of it and blast it out on your social media so that you can begin to share life and light into the hearts of others.

In this book, you will also find website addresses with resources for you to *actually use.* These web resources contain special messages, videos, songs, recordings, worksheets, and tools exclusive to the readers of this book. As you are reading, be sure to have your phone or computer handy so you can access and implement the resources at the right time with the right chapter.

I do reference God and stories from my favorite "ancient book of wisdom" (aka the Bible) within some of my stories. I want you to know I am by no means pushing my personal beliefs on you. I invite you to fill in what you need it to be in this moment where you're at. For me, as a Christ follower, God is my "higher power" and voice of truth so just know that you can insert whatever higher power you believe in during this time. My aim is to provide foundations of truth while also being "normal" (and not a weird Christian) while providing very practical knowledge for our everyday life.

#itsallgood

There is something I must warn you about…**if you agree to continue on**, we must make some agreements, because the moment you crack open the lid on your calling, there is no going back.

You won't be able to hide your little light under a bushel or ignore the call from your soul for very long.

Because of this, I have included some agreements that I invite you to participate in...

# Agreements

## (Place your hand on your heart as you read the following):

- "*I agree to remain open.*" You may resonate with some things I say, and you may not resonate with other things. Eat the fruit, spit out the seeds. Take what you wish and leave the rest...just stay open to receive what you need at that moment. And the next time you read this book, you may get an entirely new message or lesson...when you are ready, the lesson will speak right to what you need. Truth always reveals itself, even if it's at a later time.

- "*I agree to play full out.*" This means to actually dive in and use the resources that I provide. (including the spontaneous dance party ones). Faith without works is dead, so yes, fan your flame, grow your faith, *and* get into action. Action is one of the quickest ways to get out of a funk, get out of your head, and get unstuck. I am providing you with resources so that you won't have any excuses to stay where you have always been. We have work (and play) to do!

- "*I agree to enjoy the journey and keep going.*" In our instant gratification society where we microwave meals, where fast food is too slow, and where our average attention spans are now less than the attention of a gold fish (#itstrue #googleit), sllllooooowwwwwwww down and enjoy the journey. Seriously. Put this book down and look around you for 5 things that make you smile or that you are grateful for, and then keep reading. Life is a journey. Don't compare your journey with anyone else...you are exactly where you need to be.  Uncovering your purpose is a journey. It will be "all the feels" – guaranteed. This book is a journey. Of course, even in my humanness, I hope you read it in 7.5 seconds, absorb every ounce of goodness out, crank through all of the resources like a rock star and go out and conquer the world by lunchtime, then write me an awesome review or testimonial, (ooooorrrr maybe that's just what my ideal day looks like), but hey, let's be real...it...is...a...journey...it's meant to be enjoyed. It's meant to challenge you. It's meant to get you to *do the work* it takes to unpack your calling. It's meant to bring you exactly what you need when you need it, even if we don't understand it. This journey is happening *for* you. So, don't quit. Keep going. Even if it takes you the rest of your life. #seewhatIdidthere

- "*I agree to pass the flame.*" As you uncover your light and as you begin to shine, you will be compelled to share your light and the gifts you have been given with others, because there is an inner knowing that this light is not just for you. Some will accept the flame you are passing, and some won't. Just keep shining and passing it on. As you find those who will shine because you are shining, you will begin to see your tribe develop, you will see other lights be lit because of the light that you passed, and the world will—ultimately—be a brighter place.

- *"I agree to have fun!"* Smile, dance, giggle, LOL, don't take yourself (or me) too seriously. Yes, uncovering more of what we are meant for can be a serious topic, and trust me, I've been buried in the "everything in life is so official and serious and purpose driven and heavy" side of life. I've also discovered that it is one of my superpowers to – yes – dive into the deep end of the serious stuff, but to also have you laughing along the way. That's why I added in this agreement...the way we find more of what lights us up is by bringing in joy and fun! So, stand up, do your favorite dance move however awkward it may be, shake it out, laugh a bit, and then keep reading. #danceparty

Now that we are all on the same page, grab your favorite cozy mug, get comfortable in your favorite space, and get ready to be inspired, be challenged, to cry, dance, laugh, think, journal, play, discover, get into action, grow, and turn your light up.

Don't worry...we are in this together...I've gotcha...

Are you with me?

*Here we go...*

# Chapter 1
# Ready or Not...Here We Glow...

"If you bring forth what is within you, what you bring forth will save you. If you do not bring forth what is within you, what you do not bring forth will destroy you."

-Gospel According To Thomas

#WeAreMeantForMore
@CharityMajors

## Chapter 1

## Ready or Not...Here We Glow...

Now that we are a bit more acquainted (if you didn't read the introduction, I suggest you do that before reading anymore), let's dive in. Remember how I said that one of my superpowers was to dive right on into the deep end and keep you laughing along the way? Well, my friend, we are *diving in*.

I didn't always know this "divine into the deep" end was one of my superpowers. I actually thought it was something that made me feel totally awkward, out of place and like I would never find anyone else who actually wanted to have a "*real* conversation." This superpower of mine actually felt more like a curse and made me feel really alone...like I was the weird girl that wanted to have deeper conversations other than something about the weather.

Sure, "the weather is nice and it's beautiful outside. And your shoes are super cute. And I can't believe he said that, or that she posted about that. No, another dirty diaper and how much laundry?! And you have a great 30-second elevator pitch that is perfectly rehearsed that you sound just like Siri and..."

But truthfully, I despise small talk. So much so, that I have to consciously stay present and not immediately glaze over, check out, check my phone, wander off into the corner of the party to think about my vision board, the God-dream I had the night before, start running through a to-do-list or a write a future blog post (or my next book) in my head. I don't want to dabble in the shallow end. I want to dive in and have a deeper conversation.

When I say, "deeper conversation," I mean talking about hopes and dreams and ideas and strategies and breakthroughs and all the feels. Talking about what lights you up, what is holding you back, what your soul's desires are, what God is doing in your life, what you are facing right now and what you have broken through. There is nothing small or safe about those conversations, and the problem is that not everyone wants to just "dive right in."

*"Hi! I'm Charity. I believe we are all here for a reason and have a big huge purpose that will make the world a brighter place and you are here for just a time as this. Want to tell me about your hopes and dreams instead of talking about the weather?! Oh, you're walking away? Oh, ok. Yep, it's a beautiful day today. So nice to meet you!"*

What do you do when something that makes you feel alive isn't received by most of the people around you? For me, I hid my superpower away and pretended to be like everyone else.

I talked about the weather. I can recite a 30-second story like nobody's business. I can show up, smile and make small talk with the best of them.

But the problem is, it's a watered-down version of who I truly am...a mask...a dimming of my light.

Maybe you, like me, have felt this way about something that you were good at or about something that makes you feel alive. Maybe you have felt like an outcast for thinking that you are meant for more but no one else around you thinks that way or talks about it. Maybe you feel like you can't find where you belong...

I'm here to tell you that I not only know how you feel, but that you are in the right place. What I have found is that for those of us that either believe that we are *meant for more* or are starting to believe and remember that we are, it's a special type of call that has been placed on our lives. This call is not for everyone and guess what...that's ok! That's the beautiful thing about life. We all have our own individual journeys that intersect throughout life, and it is our job to follow *our* journey, towards the things that light *us* up, that make us feel *alive* inside and to follow that "*inner knowing*" - that still small voice of truth that lies within us.

But here's the thing...this special calling that is on your life also comes with some rites of passage. These rites of passages aren't always easy, either. It comes with struggles. It comes with journeying through the dark night of the soul. It comes with facing the ugly side of things that will be beautiful in the end. It comes with admitting faults, releasing blame, uncovering shame, facing fear, forgiving others, and forgiving ourselves. It comes with getting messy and doing the work of letting go of limiting beliefs, unbecoming all the things that others think we should be, moving through fear, pushing through resistance, feeling alone sometimes, and failing forward. It comes with remembering who we were created to be, who we were created by and what He says about us.

This calling is not for the faint of heart but rest assured…I know that *you have what it takes*. Even if you don't know that you do, borrow my belief. Borrow the belief that I have in you, and your journey. That you are here for a reason. That you are here, at this time, in all of eternity, *on purpose and for a purpose*. It is our job, as souls in this human experience, to uncover that purpose, to remember who we are, to follow what brings us joy and lights us up, while at the same time following the fear and resistance, and moving through those things that are trying to hold us back.

One of the main things that will try and hold us back is our ego. To understand what the ego is a bit more, let's talk about what it's not. It is *not* that still small voice inside that comes from deep within. It *is* the, sometimes, *very loud voice* that chatters a lot and tries to keep us safe. It's the limiting beliefs that tell you that you aren't enough, you don't have what it takes, not to take risks, put yourself out there or remember your truth.

Even as I type this, my ego-brain is still trying to tell me that this book isn't worth writing, and my story isn't worth telling. That this is not a topic worth shining a light on. That people will think I'm stupid for even bringing this stuff up. That I am alone in feeling this way and no one else will understand. It tells me that people will laugh at me, gossip about me, and ask, "*Who does she think she is?*" They will make fun of me, and in the end, my vulnerable and open heart will be hurt.

#wellthatsoundsawesome

#signmeupforthat

Buuuuuuuuut, *that's* how I know this message needs to come out...because, you see...despite what my inner critic says and how the lies of the darkness try and stop me, this message is not about me and and for darkness to be defeated, we must shine a light. This message, this calling on my life, has been given to me as a *gift*, not only to unwrap myself, but to pass the gift – the light - onto others...*others like you* (hence the "igniting your purpose" part of the title of this book...it ignites someone and fire spreads).

As I share the stories within this book, please understand that risking "exposure" – risking ridicule, bad reviews, airing my dirty laundry, getting real, raw and vulnerable - it's *scary*, - especially to the ego because she is here to try and keep me safe. Sharing my story exposes me and my "junk" (which, the people pleaser side of my ego is desperately trying to talk me out of writing this and pushing the save button). My ego is very justified in her safety attempts because other times in the past, when I have opened up or been vulnerable or put something "out there," it sometimes hurt me. Sometimes there were haters. Sometimes people didn't understand. Sometimes I failed. Sometimes I got rejected and hurt. And it's the ego's job to keep us safe.

Here's the thing about the ego...it's not meant to be a bad thing. She is doing exactly what she was meant to do. We were born with this innate protective mechanism, in our brain, to do whatever we can to stay alive. When we are infants, if we are rejected by our care-givers, it can ultimately lead to death. So this protection of ourselves - from being rejected - is a *good* thing. But the problem lies in the fact that this fear of rejection and death no longer serves us as adults.

What I've learned, throughout my personal journey, is the more the ego side of our brain tries to talk us out of something, the more we need to lean into that fear and "do it afraid." There's a verse in the bible that talks about how God's strength fills in the places of my weakness - the places of my "inability." I've learned that when we can use "needing courage" as a guide and move into the resistance we may be feeling, the greatest reward, passion, and purpose awaits us on the other side. I've learned that when we peel off the masks we've somehow put on, layer by layer, and open ourselves up to what it truly meant to be real and to be fully alive in this human experience, it's what truly connects us, soul to soul.

Knowing that the greatest rewards await you on the other side of being true to your divine God-given calling and walking through your fears, I want to invite you to join in the experience and conversation with us. Sharing your stories, your mistakes, your lessons, your failures, and your hurt is scary. It's vulnerable. It exposes someone in all of their weaknesses in a world that expects a person to stay strong. It reveals your flaws; it blows open the door to your heart, and it shows what goes on behind the perfect social media highlight reel.

The more real I become and the more I walk through my own fears and trust my God given purpose and intuition, there are things I learn along the way. If there's one thing I've learned, it's that anything in your life that causes you to dim your light *needs to be brought out into the light*, talked about, released, forgiven and used for good.

Even the seemingly "little wounds." Did you know there are different sizes of wounds?

Some people experience "cannon-ball" size wounds and other people experience "bullet-size" wounds. Most of us experience a combination of both. And wounds are wounds. Death by a thousand cuts still hurts. No matter the size of a wound, it hurts. One thing I've learned is if there are enough "bullet-size" wounds throughout someone's life, the emotional damage and scarring can be just as painful as a "cannon-ball" size wound. Bullet after bullet after bullet hurts just as much as one big "bang".

Cut after cut, jab after jab, these little bullets of hurt damaged my heart and caused me to shrink back, to dim my light, to play small, and to turn my "too-much" of something into not enough. These are wounds that myself and others receive throughout life's journey that cause them to dim their lights, to play small, to feel like they are not enough and the way they were made was a mistake.

I'm just going to take a guess here, but if you are reading this book, you've probably felt that same way. Like maybe you don't have what it takes, or you are "too much" for some people. Like you have to keep it all together or pretend to like surface conversations with acquaintances when all your soul really wants is to dive into the deep end with someone, hear their true heart, their hopes, their dreams, and what truly lights up their soul.

Take heart. *You are exactly where you need to be.*

This book is meant for those of us who have carried shame around the damage we received for looking or acting different than someone else.

It's meant for those of us who have heard the still small voice inside that whispers that we are *meant for more* but ignored it because we didn't know what "more" meant. Or maybe you had a glimpse into what that "more" meant, but you got stuck in fear either not knowing how to move forward or that you could actually be the one to "do the thing" that was in the vision you saw.

It's for those of us who have felt so discontent with how life is going that we either drastically change something or we feel like giving up altogether.

This message is meant for those of us who have ugly cried because we were so tired of being stuck, for those of us who have hit our head against the same ceiling time and time again believing we are meant for an open heaven, and for those of us who have limiting beliefs that hold us back but deep down don't believe them.

It's for those of us who have felt like we wanted, so desperately, to be surrounded by a tribe, and whenever we put ourselves out there and think that it could be happening, another arrow sinks into our open and vulnerable heart. So then we instinctually know that these aren't our people *yet*, so we keep wandering alone, searching and trying to find where we belong.

It's meant for those of us who have tried to step into our beautiful God given purpose, and ugly things have happened.

It's for those of us who are tired of "throwing spaghetti up against a wall" and nothing sticking, only to go back to square one, start over, and get the same frustrating non-sticky results.

It's for those of us that still believe in the good of human kind...those of us that believe we are better together, those of us that have a burning desire to serve others and show up in this life in a BIG way because we believe in a BIG God who can (and wants to do) incredible things in and through us.

It's for those of us that hear the voice inside that says our future is bigger, brighter, more abundant and beautiful than we could ever imagine.

And we can't ignore it anymore...it's time...let's go...

How do I know it's time? Because I wrote the poem below in less than 5 minutes...and when I say "I wrote," what I really mean is that it came through me – divinely inspired and given by God – I was simply the hand that had the pen and paper. As I was writing, I couldn't do anything else but revel in the flow and the perfect way that it spoke to my soul and my every heart's desire...

Have a read, because if you are raising your hand at any of the things I just wrote, this poem is for you...

### *A Call to the Light-Bearers*

Have you ever felt like
you were *meant for more* in this life?
To be and do more than go to work,
pay bills, solely be a mom or a wife?

When did you hear it?
The still small voice inside?
The one you can't shake, deny,
or from it, hide...

It's the voice that echo's,
"who are you not to be,
incredible, beautiful,
and a bright light for the world to see?

I know you're scared
and at times you feel you're "not enough..."
The hurt you have been through
and the times that were rough...

Darling, it happened FOR you,
to show you the strength you have inside.
And the light that is within you,
must come out, it can no longer hide.

The time is NOW,
not tomorrow or another day.
Not when you feel equipped
or you can see every step along the way.

It's time to shine,
to be real and connect.
Call in your sisters, your tribe,
the others whose light will reflect,

The light of the Son, His love,
His hands and feet
To a world that is broken
and so desperately needs,

The gifts you have been given,
the purpose placed in your heart.
The ones that only you have been given,
it's your time to play your part.

Step in, step up,
shine your light bright
The darkness is fleeing,
like when dawn comes after the night.

Do not be afraid or discouraged,
you have what it takes.
Be bold and courageous,

even when high are the stakes.

For I am with you and for you
and I will show you the way.
Take my hand darling.
The time to shine is now...TODAY.

The movement is building,
it cannot be contained.
The time is now,
shine your light, pass the flame.

There is a secret you already know,
your light is not meant for just you.
It's a gift you have been given to give to others,
so they can shine their light, too.

Ignite the fire,
fan your flame.
Uncover your light
and find others who are the same.

The light bringers,
the love carriers,
those who know
They are *meant for more*, too,
meant to show the world the way to go.

The way to love,
the way to unite,
the ones who will pass onto others
the internal light.

Together we can do it,
shining bright,
passing the flame...

To drive out the darkness,
to shine as one,
and make the world a brighter place.

Let's go, beautiful one.
it's time to shine,
that little light of yours
and for me to shine mine...

*All together now...*

I invite you to get the FREE Download of this poem at **CharityMajors.com/MeantForMore**.

Print it out and put it where you can remind yourself that you are a light-bearer, that it's time, that you cannot stay dim, and you are here to make the world a brighter place.

# Chapter 2
# What's Really Behind That Beautiful Selfie

> "For beautiful eyes, look for the good in others. For beautiful lips, speak only words of kindness. And for poise, walk with the knowledge that you are never alone."
>
> **Audrey Hepburn**

#WeAreMeantForMore
@CharityMajors

# Chapter 2

## What's Really Behind That Beautiful Selfie

On the surface, I am 5'10" with long blonde hair, brown eyes, clear skin, and a lean body. As an outgoing introvert, (yes, that's a thing), I am friendly, I have no problem leading a workshop or speaking in front of people, I can also be quiet at times, and need my alone time when I am running on empty. I smile – a lot (my dad said I "came out smiling") – "I like smiling. Smiling's my favorite." (See the movie "Elf" if you aren't sure what I'm talking about).

I tend to give others the benefit of the doubt (sometimes to a fault). One of my top 10-strengths in Gallup StrengthsFinders is Positivity, so I tend to see the best in others, find the good in any situation, and I love to encourage people. I also get this strength from my mom. I'm pretty sure her number one strength is Positivity. We have both been told that we live in "Positivity-La-La Land" (which was not meant to be a compliment), and, much to the dismay of my people pleasing ego, I'm *finally* okay with that. It's better than being a resident of "Debbie-Downer-Ville" if you ask me. But that's another story for another chapter.

Another thing about me is that I genuinely and wholeheartedly *love all people*. Like literally, *I love people*. I love their differences, their similarities, the shapes, colors, different gifts, different passions, different quarks, you name it, I love it. And I love you, especially for reading this book. #MeantForMoreTribe.

I graduated from high school and college with honors. I was a collegiate athlete who still holds school records to this day. I was a fitness and nutrition coach so along with my volleyball career, I am comfortable in the way I look in spandex. I am a former beauty queen, so I love a good dress with lots of bling and have learned to do my hair, makeup, and work a stage with the best of them.

As a speaker, author, writer and entrepreneur that gets to be my own boss and work from anywhere, my offices have included beaches in Mexico, beautiful parks, and my kitchen table (wearing sweats and slippers while my kiddo runs around chasing the cat). I absolutely *love* being an entrepreneur. I always have. I say this not to brag, but to share some of the "outside stuff" that I've accomplished to give you a comparison of what can really be happening on the inside (stay tuned for that part). I have worked *really hard*, I've thrown so much "spaghetti at the wall only to have nothing stick," I've had *plenty* of wall kicking moments and I have failed more than I have succeeded, but I'm proud of what I've accomplished so far...(half the time I'm not even sure how I did it)! And I know *there's still more* in store for me to build, create, launch, write and figure out...

My husband is one of the hottest men you will ever see in your life. Combine Gerard Butler and Matthew McConaughey together, and you now have the visual of what my husband looks like #hubbahubba. He was the guy that about 100 girls "just knew" they were going to marry. He is a firefighter (Hello, Mr. July!), he is a musician (I get to go home with the lead singer of the band), and he is the perfect balance of strong and gentle, funny and kind. He supports me with my (lots of) crazy ideas, we adventure all around the world, he thinks I am most beautiful in my sweat pants and no make-up, he is a *great* dad, and he makes me laugh every single day. See why they all wanted to marry him? (Sorry girls, God had different plans in mind...).

Our marriage is, by *no means* perfect...we have disagreements, we've been to counseling, we are very different in a lot of ways, but I wholeheartedly know that we belong together and I'm so grateful God brought us together for all of the ups and down of life.

Our son, Judah, is as handsome as they come, as sweet as can be, and he lights up whatever room he walks into. If you have ever taken Gallup StrengthsFinder, you'll know what I mean when I say that "his *woo* is high." (More on this test later).

I became a successful entrepreneur, community influencer, and activist through a *lot* of hard work and dedication. It's something I am proud of because I truly feel in alignment with my God given purpose when I am loving, leading, and serving others.

From the outside, looking in, there is nothing ugly about my life. It's all beauty, butterflies, and cute babies. #blessed

Being a former Beauty Queen, you may think I'm going to write about beauty hacks, fashion tips, photoshop tutorials, and how to take the perfect selfie (especially from the title of this chapter). Don't get me wrong. I think all those tools are good to use and if it's right for you, use them to the best of your ability. I'm a firm believer in beauty, inside and out, so be sure to check out the resources page and blog at **www.CharityMajors.com** for some of my favorite tricks and tools to the things I just mentioned. But remember, I'm the "dive into the deep end" kinda girl...so here we jump again!

In this chapter, we will be discussing "beauty." I am talking about a specific kind of beauty, though. Not the surface kind, so let's dive in. The interesting thing about this word is the disconnect between what society says is beautiful, and what we, as human souls, *perceive* to be beautiful.

This discussion is stemming from (not just because it's an innate desire for us, as women, to be beautiful and to be seen as that), but what print and media defines as beauty, and the *disconnect* we, as humans and spiritual beings, ***feel*** to be beautiful.

Webster defines beauty as: *"the quality or aggregate of qualities in a person or thing that gives **pleasure to the senses** or **pleasurably exalts the mind or spirit** (emphasis added); a particularly graceful, ornamental, or excellent quality; a brilliant, extreme, or egregious example or instance."*

*"The quality or qualities in a person or thing that gives **pleasure to the senses or pleasurably exalts the mind or spirit**.*" How's that for a definition? Let's break this down and dig a little deeper. Let's start with the senses.

Our five senses consist of sight, smell, taste, feel, and hearing.

Did you know that there are actual physical qualities and measurements that our eyes are drawn to (aka the sense of sight)? Things like symmetry in a face, clarity of skin, a healthy body, a smile, and good posture? (1)

The media and print magazines clearly utilize what our eyes can see as one of their main ways to convey beauty… hence photoshop or apps filled with filters to give clear skin and symmetrical lines in a face, along with the ideal image of long luscious hair and a trim waist-line. But what about those of us who aren't a cover model with a photoshop guy sitting in our office waiting to airbrush our every selfie? See what I mean by "disconnect?"

On the other end of the "definition of beauty" spectrum is the "pleasurably exalts the mind or spirit" part of Webster's definition. With this in mind, I created a Facebook poll that asked what people believed that makes someone beautiful. Comments consisted of things like "being kind," "gratitude," "helping others," "being happy," "confidence," and the like. Not one person out of the dozens of comments I received said anything about a physical trait. #Hmmm…

I started to ask myself, if Webster's definition includes the five senses and science shows that we are attracted to symmetry, why is it that people's answers on my Facebook poll had nothing to do with physical attributes? And why is it that print media and trending social media applauds and encourages the physical attributes like a thigh gap, long fake eye lashes, a tiny Barbie waste, and puckered lips? (Can we *please* be done with the duck face already? This trait of big full lips is being encouraged to the point that teenage girls are injuring their lips by putting them into shot glasses, sucking so hard it breaks blood vessels and their lips swell. #thishasgottostop).

Another question I started to wonder about was why are we (especially as girls and women), so focused on the ugly things when it comes to our beautiful souls? We focus on our "not enough-ness." The parts of us we want to change or enhance because of the beauty standards we are bombarded with every single day. Where is the disconnect between what the media says is beautiful and what we truly *feel* and *know* to be beautiful? Where is the beauty that we experience that lies within each and every human being that God created? And why does society place such a high price on the outward appearance? (welcome to my crazy brain)...

*Experiencing* someone else's beauty (not just seeing it) goes deeper than just what you perceive with your eyes (and it's deeper than what the media shoves down our throats as their standard of beauty...and yes, all of this *is* coming from a former beauty queen). It has to do with how one's deeper understanding, also known as the subconscious, interprets those physical qualities. Whether you know it (or believe it), your subconscious is not only pumping blood through your body, blinking your eyes without having to think about it, and causing your lungs to transport oxygen and remove carbon dioxide, but it's also interpreting external data at every moment; *over 80,000 interpretations of the world around you* at any given moment, to be exact.

The subconscious mind interprets signals in others like their scent and pheromones, the shape of their body, the health of their smile and teeth and mouth, length and quality of hair and nails, and the whites of their eyes. When someone has skin blemishes, the subconscious interprets that as unhealthy on the inside, and it comes out through the skin. Interesting, right?!

The subconscious interprets other things we can't see (or may not even be aware of) like another person's energy or the "vibration" they give off. Have you ever been around a "Debbie downer" and felt the need to get as far away from them as possible? Or maybe you've seen a creepy guy and felt like you needed to go take a shower and clean off the creepiness? #yeahmetoo Your subconscious picks up on the energies and vibrations of everyone and everything around you. Now, before you write this completely off as "woo-woo," let's learn more...

Our brains have what's called "mirror-neurons," meaning that hundreds of millions of little neurons in our brain pick up on the actions of those around us and begin to mirror those actions and behaviors. Have you ever been around someone whose smile is contagious? Or yawned after someone else yawned? Those are your mirror-neurons doing their job.

All of these signals and vibrations around us are too much for the conscious mind to handle at one time, so all this interpretation happens at a deeper subconscious level – a level you aren't even aware of...

*Until you are.*

Now, stick with me here if you aren't the "vibin'" type and let's take you back to science class and learn a little bit about physics and energy. If you can remember far enough back to science class, you may recall that everything on the planet is made up of atoms. *Atoms have either a positive (+) or negative (-) charge.* When you pair atoms together, you get the elements of everything around us. (Remember the Periodic Table of Elements?) Hydrogen ($H_2O$ = two (+) hydrogen atoms and one (-) oxygen atom), aluminum, chromium, platinum, uranium, and all the other ones I don't remember... #sorryMrGlick

Every cell of your body is paired together with atoms, giving it a certain "charge" or "frequency". The higher the frequency, the more conscious and alive the object is. For example, a tree is made up of all its special combination of atoms and has a higher vibration than my sunglasses, which has its own special combination of atoms that make up the plastic, metal screws, and lenses. (and yes, I am looking at things around me as I type this and using them as examples...I told you my office was at the beach sometimes)!

Here is another example that you probably have heard of. "Alive food" or raw food is more "living" than cooked, processed, or packaged food. A fresh carrot out of the ground has a higher frequency or vibration than a boiled carrot, and it definitely has a higher frequency than another food that is orange - cheese puffs. Why is the raw carrot vs. the cooked carrot vs. the cheese puff different? Because the boiling water and the heat changed the frequency of the molecules that made up the carrot and it changed its physical properties and vibration. And cheese puffs? Well, let's just say that there is nothing natural, high vibe or alive about those little, neon orange, finger staining, stays fresh for 47 years, little buggers. Make sense?

#keephangingwithme

There are ways to raise and lower your personal frequency or vibration. Everything that you do, every single day, affects that. Obviously, we all are vibrating. Some of that vibration depends on what you have put *into* your body, which feeds your cells, cells then divide and create more cells that continue to create your body. Is your body made up of cheese puffs and the chemicals in soda or are your cells made up of living foods like greens, lean organic meats, herbs and organic ancient grains? This will be reflected in your body and in how invigorated you feel every day.

As a former nutrition specialist, this is the part that I tell you that "you are what you eat, so don't be easy, cheap, or fake." I have included some of my favorite healthy and easy recipes in the resources for this chapter, so be sure to visit **CharityMajors.com/MeantForMore.**

More importantly than me getting on a nutrition soap box, is me getting on a "this is your life's calling and you only get one body to carry out that calling" soap box.

As we established before, it takes a special soul to come into this world, at this exact time, and start to uncover and live into their life's bigger purpose in order to make the world a better place. The bible calls this "bringing heaven to earth" and I'm here for it. And since you are reading this book, you are included in this category. You, my friend, only get *one body* to carry out this special calling of being a light-bearer, a culture catalyst, a world changer. If you are not taking care of your body by eating natural clean food, limiting sugar intake, drinking at least half your body weight of water in ounces, getting adequate rest and staying active, you are doing yourself a disservice. You are doing your divine calling a disservice. You are doing a disservice to those that could be impacted by the big hopes and dreams that are in your heart. You are doing a disservice to the Creator of the universe and galaxies, the Creator of our beautiful planet and the Creator of your soul.

God did not make us to walk around tired and foggy headed all day. We, as ones who are here on purpose for a purpose, are not meant to carry extra weight that slows the body down and strains its internal organs. We shouldn't be winded when walking upstairs or playing with our kids. We shouldn't be foggy headed and not able to think clearly. We need our bodies functioning optimally. We need our bodies to serve us well and not hold us back. They should help us carry our calling, not inhibit it.

I want to encourage you to take a good hard look at how you are caring for this one body you have been given. You are meant to nourish and honor your body so that it helps propel you into every level of your God-given purpose. Love your body enough to take care of it. Are you feeding it with clean nutrient rich foods that will transfer their high vibrating frequency into your cells? (and yes, you know which ones I'm talking about…remember the carrot vs. the cheese puff)? Are you giving your body the purified hydration that it needs to function optimally and provide your body with energy? (I guarantee when you increase your water intake, you will have a boost in energy, your skin will glow, your body will release toxins and "fluffiness" better, and you will sleep better). Are you giving your body adequate rest, at night, as well as throughout different cycles and seasons of what's going on in your life?

Sleep is one of the easiest ways to allow your body to rejuvenate. When we sleep, our body gives off chemicals that allow our body to repair, burn off cortisol, which allows your body to burn fat better and it also curbs your appetite.

Adequate sleep helps improve memory, it helps curb inflammation, it increases your creativity, it improves performance, improves attention span and capacity to learn new things, it helps you lower and manage stress better, helps you be less irritable, and be in a better mood.

I hope by now, you are getting the point...get your rest! Even if you have to set an alarm to remind yourself to go to bed before 11pm, do it.

Now that we have established the importance of rest and what we put *into our bodies* and how it affects the way our body vibrates, as I'm sure you know, how we *move* our bodies also matters. Remember when you learned in science class that "a body at rest stays at rest and a body in motion stays in motion?" Have you ever experienced the momentum of when you start working out, you are more motivated to keep working out? And isn't the starting always the hardest? It's because of this principle. I encourage you to find exercises, activities, classes, and a lifestyle that encourages you to *stay in motion.*

When I was a personal trainer, I always suggested that clients find the activities that they would actually *do* on a regular basis. It isn't about needing to fit into a "fitness box" and doing something because someone else is. It's about finding an activity, a class, a way to stay active, and a group of people that will be a part of your fitness community. I personally love pilates and barre, resistance training in the gym, being active outside with activities like bike riding, golf, volleyball and snowboarding. I also try to tune into my body to see what I feel like I am needing. It may be that I need a 10-class pass to barre class or a 3-month membership at a spin studio. I may choose to jog in the spring or join a HIIT class at my gym. I also listen to my body when it comes to the natural ebbs and flows of the menstrual cycle. I encourage you to do the same. Did you know there are ways to honor your cycle and the hormonal changes when it comes to activity and even our schedules? (You can watch my vlog series on this topic at **CharityMajors.com/blog/finding-flow**) for more on this *very enlightening* topic.

I encourage you to try new things, try new classes, have a dance party in your living room, (or even have a dance party right now), test out different workout styles and see which ones fit you best within a certain season of what your body is needing and longing for for that time. This concept of healthy activity also means that you need to honor and listen to your body. Your body is a divine masterpiece and you intuitively *know* when something is right for you. This isn't an excuse to not workout hard sometimes (because even I don't always like to do that)...this is an invitation to really tune in and listen to the energy and seasonal ebbs and flows of your body and honor them by matching appropriate activity that will support you and the call on your life. Busy seasons may need softer and more relaxing fitness routines while other times, intense and heavy weights are a better fit.

Movement is one of the best ways to increase your vibration, energy, how you feel and it's even better when we can connect the body and the mind. When we understand that there are emotional or mental blocks that we can't quite get "unstuck," from, we have the gift of getting our body moving. It is a beautiful technique that can help in ways we don't even know.

For me, when I am feeling low in energy or even when I need a boost in my mindset or some inspiration, one of my favorite things (besides reading the Bible) is to pop in an audio book or inspirational podcast, get my muscles moving at the gym, and like magic, when I'm done, I am at a high state for creativity! It's where some of my best ideas have come from and was actually a routine I regularly did to write this book. (Need a good podcast? Check out mine, called "Meant For More" at **CharityMajors.com/podcast**).

The point is to find something that works for you. Find something that makes you *feel good*. Fitness and moving your body should be fun, enjoyable, and sustainable for the rest of your life.

Besides just how we move our bodies and what we fuel our bodies with, what goes *into our minds* has a huge effect on the energy signals we put out to the world…bigger than you may think, and studies are finally showing evidence of this. If you think about it, #punintended, our brain and central nervous system operates on tiny nerve signals that are electric in nature. Electric. Electricity. Signals. Radio waves. Get the connection and where I'm going with this? #Vibes.

Did you know that certain thoughts and states of mind have different frequencies and that it has actually been measured? States of gratitude, peace, courage, love, abundance and joy vibe at a much higher frequency than states of fear, grief, apathy, anger, shame, and scarcity. There's a reason the Bible says to "renew your mind" and to "focus on things that are pure, good, and lovely..." Science proves this stuff!

The word "emotion" derives from the Latin root "emotere," where "e" means "out" and "movere" means "to move." So, etymologically, "emotion" literally means "to move out" or "movement." When we feel something like anger- we are to feel it and move it out (want to go to be active yet?!)

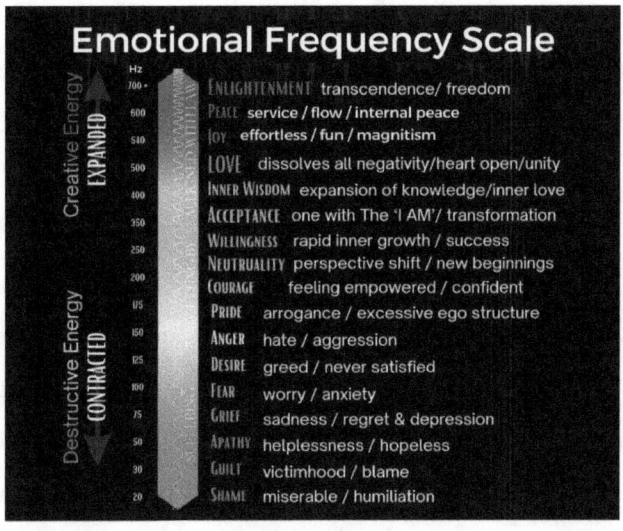

This chart shows the measured vibration frequencies in Hz of these states of being and emotions. (2) Now, you may be wondering what this chart has to do with anything beautiful and how we originally started this chapter. This chart and these frequencies or vibrations have to do with how we experience others **and** how they *experience us*. How their subconscious interprets our personal frequency and state of being.

Remember the second part of Webster's definition of Beauty? "The quality or aggregate of qualities in a person or thing that gives pleasure to the senses or **pleasurably exalts the mind or spirit.**"

This is that. Exalting, lifting up, raising up the mind or spirit. High vibrational frequencies. Enlightenment (this is wisdom or understanding). Joy. Love. Reason. Acceptance. Willingness (or being open). Courage. Neutrality (not being triggered or seeing things from all angles and being okay with others' differences of opinion). Gratitude. Peace. This is where the good stuff is. This is where, when we operate from these spaces, others "feel" who we are, and they are captivated by it. When the state of our minds are settled on and coming from a place kindness and love. When our very *being* emits peace, acceptance, clarity, openness and service.

When we operate from these higher vibrational states of being, studies show that *literally*, the vibration of our brain and the vibration of our heart *align*. Our neurology and physiology are connected. Our head and our heart align. And there is power in alignment. The dictionary defines alignment as "the correct position or positioning of different components relative to one another so that they perform properly."

Take a look at the following chart and what happens to our heart rate when we are feeling anxious, worried, irritated and frustrated. I don't know about you, but I've absolutely felt the tightness in my chest, the sleepless nights and the racing mind that happens. And on the other hand, look at the softer rhythm of. the heart when there are positive emotions, gratitude, love, care, when we are supported and supporting others...I've also felt the peace, groundedness, focus and openness of these feelings in my body as well.

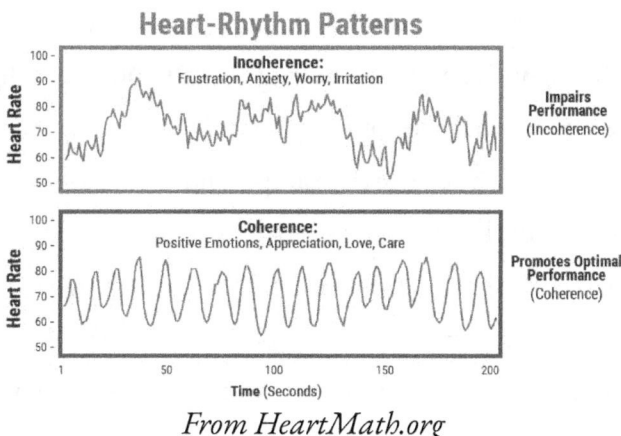

*From HeartMath.org*

Being in a state of healthy emotional states of beings and alignment leaves us and others with a feeling – *an experience of the essence of who you are.* They remember it. They like the way they feel around a person in that state. They post on a social media thread that these qualities and characteristics are what makes a person beautiful

When you get your body into that state, you literally vibrate and radiate true beauty. True magnitism. Peace. Your presence makes an impression. No photoshop filters, no unattainable standard from print media, no sucking your lips through a shot glass. Just raw, real, radiant beauty, vibrating from every cell in your being, pulsing from your soul. The way it should be.

#Beautiful.

It is our job, as flawed by growth-minded humans, to bring our body, on a daily (and sometimes moment by moment) basis, into alignment and up to these healthy emotional states of being. It's also our job, as light-bearers, to not only intentionally set our hearts and mind on things above, and choose our thoughts, but to be an example and encourage others to do the same. That's one of the ways we can collectively make the world a brighter place. Too many people let their thoughts run the show when we should take every thought captive. We have the choice in what we think, believe, and the foundation of truth we decide to build upon. Are you choosing to live from a place of shame and fear about a situation or are you allowing God to heal those places of hurt and provide His perspective, which allows you to live from a place of love and forgiveness?

Now that you have a better understanding of energy, there are things that you can do, on a daily basis, that help your state of being so that you begin to allow others to be impacted by your very presence. Like I mentioned, these things include inner healing of wounds (however big or small they are), prayer, journaling, gratitude, clean eating, staying hydrated, and removing toxicity from your body, living an active life, and living a life of purpose, in alignment with your purpose.

Because I am passionate about being in alignment, and the ripple effect of more of us living from a place of love, peace, healing and wholeness instead of brokenness, shame and fear, I have included ways to align your body and heart, a guided journaling and meditation recording, fitness and nutrition tips within this chapter's resources at **CharityMajors.com/MeantForMore**.

# Chapter 3
# When Life Isn't All Rainbows & Glitter

> "Your hardest times often lead to the greatest moments of your life."
>
> -Charity Majors
>
> #WeAreMeantForMore
> @CharityMajors

# Chapter 3

## When Life Isn't All Rainbows & Glitter

We learned all about the awesome vibrational and emotional states and how we should make it a daily practice to be in states of love, joy, peace, gratitude, and more (if you're a Christ-follower, you should be recognizing the fruits of the Spirit #lightbulb). But what about the times where we aren't in those states of being? What about the times when we don't choose love, or something happens to us that draws out what's really underneath and triggers us?

The shame? Fear? Apathy? Pride? Anger? Guilt? Grief? What happens when we are coming from a place of these lower vibrational states of being? What happens to your body, mind, and how does it affect those around us? This "low vibe space" is a part of the "head model" of the personal development world that most people try and mantra themselves out of. And don't get me wrong, I love me some identity statements, and affirmations and use them on a regular basis. They are a great way to begin to reprogram the conversation going on in our heads and to remind us of who we truly are. Our thoughts come from our beliefs, which then create our actions, then our habits and ultimately our destiny, so please, use mantras and affirmations...I'm just suggesting that there is more to this puzzle...

Outside of this "head model" for personal development, there is a new and deeper understanding – the "heart model" – that is beginning to take hold. (Spiritual Intelligence is also another dimension of this, but that's another conversation for another day). Back to this heart model, which includes *acknowledging* that these feelings exist (instead of pretending they aren't there, which – at least for me - affirmations can sometimes feel like), and with that acknowledgement of those feelings, we head straight into the places of our darkness so we can begin to shine a light, detach from them and insert new and empowering beliefs.

In July of 2017, I was in the lowest of the low. I went through one of the most painful experiences of my life - painful in body, mind, and to the deepest level of my being.

I experienced a miscarriage.

I was almost 12 weeks pregnant with a little soul, heartbeat, and life within me. This baby was a surprise to my husband and me, but we embraced the adventure (of what would have been 2 kids under the age of two) with joy, gratitude, a little bit of "*holy crap, here we go,*" and excitement. I was healthy, active, had a flawless first pregnancy, and beautiful homebirth with our first son. So, although miscarriage was a passing thought in my mind because "it's always a possibility and that's why people don't post on social media until after 12 weeks," the thought of losing our baby wasn't really on my radar.

Until it was.

It wasn't *supposed to be* in the plan for *our* family.

Until it happened.

And it happened in one of the worst ways. I experienced much of the process of a miscarriage – not at home in a safe and private place – but in a very public place, with all eyes on me and nowhere else to go.

My husband, Chris, my one-year old son (at the time), Judah and my mom (thank God for family who can come along and help take care of a kiddo while traveling) were on a trip. It was a quick little weekend getaway to relax, enjoy the lake and mountains, and reconnect. I had started spotting a little bit, and although our midwives were supportive, positive and encouraging, intuitively I...just...knew...

Ever had that feeling – that inner, intuitive knowing – that despite what others may be saying, you...just...*know*?

The bleeding I had started to experience, along with the trust I had in my intuition led to a trip to a midwifery's clinic in the town we were visiting. I remember it so vividly, as we met the midwife that we were referred to (because we were out of town), and anxiously awaiting the results of the ultrasound. My mind raced, my hand clenched onto my husbands, and then we heard... We heard not the sounds of the baby's heartbeat...the same one we had heard just a few weeks earlier...but the sound of the voice of the midwife, as she regretfully told us, "there is no heartbeat..."

In a split second, my own heart shattered into a million pieces as I began to cry and couldn't do anything else but collapse into my husband's arms. It wasn't just my eyes and emotions that were crying. It was my heart and soul. Every part of my being was grieving this loss.

The dreams we had envisioned of our little family, the prayers I had prayed over this little life, the hopes and dreams that come along with the gift of a child - all ripped away in an instant with the simple words of, "there isn't a heartbeat."

Driving back to our hotel with tears streaming down our faces, and the song "It Is Well with My Soul" ironically playing on the radio, we decided to pack up and catch the next flight home. Within a couple hours, we could be at home in a safe and comfortable place, while my body went through the process of the miscarriage.

We made it to the airport as my cramping and bleeding increased. We *desperately* prayed that the 53-minute flight would be short enough so we could make it home.

It wasn't.

In all of my pain, cramping, tears, and being at the point of almost passing out, I was trapped at the front of an airplane having one of the worst experiences of my life in front of every passenger.

I was taking trips every 5 minutes to the tiny and weird smelling restroom at the front of the plane...it was humiliating, exposing, vulnerable and felt so isolating. Bleeding through my pants, sweating profusely and being in visible pain while crying, I felt shame like I had never known before. The constant looks from other passengers and questions from the flight attendants wondering what was going on seared into my breaking heart and soul.

I felt helpless, broken, and trapped. I felt afraid and alone, despite my husband's best attempts to comfort me, hold me, stroke my hair, and get me cranberry juice. All I wanted was to be at home, in our safe place, where I could process the loss of our child in a way that I felt comfortable (or as comfortable as one can be in that situation).

After what was the longest 53-minute flight of my life, we landed and immediately drove to our midwifery center where we received care and compassion throughout the rest of the process.

I was told that physical and emotional healing would be a process, and I should continue to rest. What they didn't tell me was that I wouldn't want to get out of bed in the morning and that I would question God's faithfulness and goodness in the midst of this horrible thing.

What I didn't know was why it happened and what the purpose behind it was. What I didn't know was that this was my dark night of the soul…

*"What was wrong with me? What did I do wrong? Why?"* Questions - the BIG ones - that only God has the answer to, filled my mind.

What I didn't know was that I would also then feel fear with my perfect and healthy child and how my mind would run to the worst case scenarios. *"Is he going to choke on that food? Is he going to fall and break his neck? Is he going to wake up in the morning? Is someone going to take him from me? What if I can't keep him safe? Am I failing as a mom? Is he going to die too?"*

These made up stories that my mind raced through always ended up with him dying, or that I would feel like I was drowning in shame and guilt that there was something wrong with me and my body. I didn't know such dark places existed, but I experienced them with every cell of my body and soul.

I questioned God, I questioned myself, my purpose, the purpose of life, why it's even worth it, and why I was even living. Most of my thoughts began to stem from a place of fear, anger, grief, apathy, brokenness and shame.

The lowest of the low vibrations, all at once, without any light at the end of the tunnel.

I remember one day shortly after the loss of our baby, I was ugly crying on the bathroom floor, with salty tears running down my face, asking the *big* questions and crying out to God. In the midst of all of the brokenness I felt, the shame I was drowning in, and how alone I felt, God came and met me on that cold tile floor. His wrap around presence brought peace like I'd never known. He sat with me and let me know I wasn't alone. And instead of a "7-step to get out of my shame" plan, He gave me the unique perspective that we are all created with such divine intention, for a purpose, on purpose and not one of us is a mistake. He began to heal the deepest parts of me that no earthly modality can do.

Maybe you, like me, have experienced feelings like this. Maybe you too, have been through your dark night of the soul. Maybe you too felt overwhelmed by shame. The feeling of not wanting to get out of bed. Feeling like there is something wrong with you. Or maybe it was anger. Lack of understanding. Questioning whether it is worth even living another day...me too friend...me too.

It is within our deepest, darkest times and where the most pressure can be applied, that what's on the inside will come to the surface. Within this deep place of darkness, my shame, my anger, my grief, and my brokenness that I had buried deep down, surfaced.

Knowing I couldn't go through this alone, (despite my husband's best efforts, and he was *amazing* through the entire process, it's just that his processing and grief was different than mine), I sought help through pastoral care and a grief and trauma counselor. I knew that this deep seeded, soul shattering brokenness wasn't something that I could "affirmation" my way out of, and I needed professional help and deep inner healing. The counselor began a therapy called EMDR, which is a light and sound technique that allows the right side of your brain and the left side of your brain to connect on a high level. This brain connection allows the person having the EMDR treatment to pay attention to the patterns, stories, and body sensations that connect to the tragedy they are processing through.

It was a very interesting and enlightening process to say the least. Because of how our brain works, other instances in my past where I experienced other feelings of shame or brokenness showed up as well. Our brain connects similar feelings to similar neuron pathways. It's kind of like a plate of spaghetti. One story will intertwine with others and create a big plate of intertwined signals that are connected. So not only did we work on processing through, detaching and reframing from the tragedy of the miscarriage that triggered uncontrollable emotions, we were able to untangle a lot of other past hurts that were connected as well.

Through my therapy and inner healing, I finally found relief through the process, the uncontrollable emotions became manageable as they lost their hold on me and the trigger began to subside. As God came into those deep places and helped heal and speak Truth, I was able to see the gifts in the hardest of times. My brain untangled the knots of the trauma, almost like a massage therapist works on a knot in a muscle. I was healing by going straight through my grief, instead of stuffing it, ignoring it, or achieving my way out of it (like I had done in the past). I was healing because I was letting The Healer do what He does best.

This book – my story - is also part of my healing, and it is my hope that through the messiness that I have experienced and the healing that I have experienced, that it can provide hope and inspiration to someone else who may be going through a dark time of their own.

Through processing of the loss of what both Chris and I sensed was a little girl, I began to see some light breaking through my darkness. I again began to believe in, and draw upon, not only God, my family and community, but in my God given strengths. One of my strengths is Positivity, which means that I can find the best in any situation and in any person. I began to, although painfully and I admittedly wanted to just wallow in my bed and not do anything some days, I began to intentionally search for the good in this soul shattering situation. I began to see how the life of my daughter, even though she was only meant for heaven, was a life enveloped in love. She was a surprise, and surprise gifts are surrounded with joy. She knew only love, joy and belonging without ever having to experience the opposite of those things, which so many of us experience in this human experience. She had an assignment, and however short it was, it made an impact on me for eternity.

I began to see how grateful I was for my healthy son and the miracle that he *truly* is. I began to see how *every single person* on the planet is a beautiful miracle. I began to see people differently. I began to replace the deep seeded shame with an even deeper seeded love and grace for every...single...person. Including you. Even as I write this, I imagine you reading it, and my heart is filled with so much gratitude and love for you because you, beautiful one, are *such...a...miracle...*

Did you know that there are millions of pieces and parts of DNA and cells and atoms that must perfectly align and come together for life to be sustained?

My son is a living, breathing, walking miracle. I am a living, breathing, walking miracle. *You* are a living, breathing, walking miracle. What a revelation to have and I truly believe it with *every* ounce of my being.

Through this tragedy, I gained a new level of understanding of how every single human is a beautiful miracle and beautiful creation. I began to feel overwhelming gratitude for life and for those around me. I was able to use how this tragedy triggered other feelings that were below the surface, and get help needed for the emotional untangling process, so they had less of a hold of me. This began to change everything...

I began to process through the shame and the brokenness of my past and take another step into my God given power and purpose. The words you are reading are part of that. Sharing this story is a part of my healing. Sharing the light that comes out of darkness is part of my purpose, and although I will never "arrive," I am stepping forward, in faith, believing that there is a gift in every situation and power in sharing stories of healing and hope on the other side of tragedy. I am intentionally choosing to draw out the nuggets of gold and worth, so that I can share them with you. I believe that in me sharing my story, it gives others permission to do the same. Did you know that the word "testimony" in the bible means "God do it again?" And I believe that as I share the healing I've received, God *will* do it again.

I will admit, sharing the hardest parts of our stories may not be easy at first, but it is *always* worth it. It's what connects us, heart to heart, soul to soul, in our human-ness and lets others know that we are not alone.

I want to encourage you that if you, like me, have experienced the brokenness and hurt that one can experience through life, through loss, through abuse, through misunderstanding, through false perception, or whatever it may be, to follow those promptings and trails of hurt, to do the work needed to heal, invite God into those places and as you heal, to *share your story*. Your story *matters*. The lessons you have been given are not for you to keep to yourself. Being brave, open and vulnerable actually shows your *strength* and encourages others to do the same. And God can do what He did in your life in the lives of others.

Whether part of your personal journey is to seek God, professional help, getting a coach, pastoral care, inner healing or even learning things such as EFT (Emotional Freedom Technique), I encourage you to do it. EFT is an amazing technique that you can do at any time with no equipment needed. The technique combines acknowledging how you are feeling, and utilizes the tapping of meridian points on your body that "tell" your body "you're safe," all while using positive psychology verbiage. Pairing the positive psychology with the tapping techniques that tell your body you are safe creates major healing shifts after just a few self-sessions. This is a technique I utilize on a regular basis for many areas of my life (including stress, anxiety, and overwhelm) and you're even able to use it when something triggers a new level of shame, self-worth, doubt, or fear. It's a great technique to learn and one that I highly recommend doing.

I have included some resources about this within this chapter at **CharityMajors.com/MeantForMore**.

It is *your assignment and part of your purpose,* to go into the dark places and get the help you need to heal them so that you can shine brighter and show up in the world in a bigger and bolder way. The work can be hard, but the growth, freedom, alignment and authenticity that comes from it is a freedom like you've never felt.

Besides the professional help and Emotional Freedom Technique, another form of healing comes when we share our stories. I found it healing not only to share our story of loss with other families within support groups, through journaling as well as in a collaborative book I am writing with other families who have also experienced the tragedy of losing a child.

There is power in getting a story "up and out," not in the way of gossip, but in the way of processing for greater understanding and bringing something out from the darkness and into the light. Once it is in the light, it begins to lose its power. It begins to loosen its hold on you. You can begin the healing process, but only when you have the courage to go to the places where that story of shame or disgrace, of not enough, of being too much, of not having what it takes, of being broken, of whatever that limiting belief may be, and disconnect from that emotional attachment. Allow God to come in and share His perspective on the situation and ask Him who He is revealing Himself to be to you.

The more we process through something, the less tangled up it is in our thoughts. This external processing can be things like talk therapy, journaling, joining a support group, or finding a safe place for you to work through the tangles.

We all have a story to tell and it can only be told in the way that you can tell it from your experience. I invite you to begin to surround yourself with those who will embrace your "too much," and your bright shining light, along with the dark side that we all have. We can't journey through this alone, so find those who will hold a safe space for you to heal but who also won't let you stay where you've been.

Find those who will love you, even in your darkest moments, and share the hope of the light on the other side. Find those who will draw the best out of you—draw out the love and joy and peace and gratitude, courage and wisdom. And those people or experiences that reveal the triggers and places of shame, anger, apathy, etc… those are there for a reason, too. It is meant to be a clue to show you where you need healing, where you can do the work on your heart and soul (and it may take professional help), so that you can begin to offer the same healing and hope for others.

If you need a safe place, you can join the Meant For More FREE Facebook group at **CharityMajors.com/MeantForMoreTribe.**

And to those of you who have experienced loss, whether it is a child, maybe it was the loss of a job or a marriage or a friend or hopes and dreams, I invite you to find the gold nuggets among the dirt. To find the diamonds made from the pressure. Find the gifts within the resistance. You are strong enough and you will make it through this. This gold, this strength, this value, this worth, *It's within you*. It always has been. And God wastes nothing. It's up to you to embrace the pressure of life and develop into the beautiful bright shining light that is within you so that the world around you can be bright and beautiful too.

> *Because darkness cannot drive out darkness. Only light can.*
> *Hate cannot drive out hate. Only love can...*
>
> Martin Luther King, Jr.

I invite you to take a moment and listen to the song, "*It is Well,*" under this chapter's resources at **CharityMajors.com/MeantForMore**. It was an encouragement to my soul that even in the middle of a storm, that God can use everything for good, and that it truly *is* well with my soul.

This is also my prayer for you.

# Chapter 4

# Put on Your Mud Boots

> "True forgiveness is when you can say 'Thank you for that experience.'"
>
> -Oprah Winfrey
>
> #WeAreMeantForMore
> @CharityMajors

# Chapter 4

# Put on Your Mud Boots

Imagine a swamp. Tall trees, tangled bushes, weird smells, creepy sounds, and mucky water that you have to sludge through without knowing what's below the surface. #freaksmeout

Shame and Vulnerability expert, Brene Brown, calls shame the swampland of the soul. (If you haven't seen her TedTalk on Shame and Vulnerability, it's a must watch. I have linked it in this chapter's resources at **CharityMajors.com/ MeantForMore**). Guess what, Beautiful One? Even though it's not the sexiest of topics, put your mud boots on because we are diving right in with this chapter (I told you we were diving into the deep end...but don't worry, we will come up for air and laugh, too)...

#Shame

I'm sharing about this "not-so-sexy" topic because I believe it is the root of a lot of fears that we attach limiting beliefs to and how we dim our lights. Are you with me? Strap those boots on my friend...Here we go...

My stomach was in knots. I was humiliated. I was puzzled and did the "palm to the face" move multiple times. My heart was puzzled and hurt to hear that my best friend (at the time) had publicly shamed me. She had not only socially and publically trash talked me and the new friends I had made, but she put down the *entire* pageant industry. #PageantProblems. And it was all over social media for the world to see. I didn't understand. (insert the palm to the face move again). She had been the friend that came with me to try on dresses and cheered me on from the audience when I competed for the first time.

She told me she believed in me day after day, when I decided to compete and as I prepared for the actual competition. She met some of the amazing women I was getting to know and had become friends with and saw how great they were. Women who were supportive, encouraging, active in the community and fun, compared to the typical stereotype of catty and snobby pageant women that so many people have.

I'll admit, before deciding to join a pageant I, too, had a perception of "pageant girls" and that they were just pretty girls in dresses competing against each other. A lot of people have that perception...maybe you do too. It's ok...but it also raises a gut check as to why women feel the need to stereotype, in a negative way...(more on this later). Keep reading with an open mind and be willing to open up to a new perspective.

After actually joining a pageant, getting to know the women and seeing what they were about, I can *truly* say that they are some of the kindest, most service oriented and driven women I have ever met. They are founders of non-profits, they are speakers, authors, community activists, military women, teachers, moms, and they *intentionally chose* to join something that causes them to grow and become a better person while serving their community. They are some of the bravest women I have ever met, some of the kindest women I know, and some of the most accomplished women I have ever been around.

(Side note - if you personally, want to challenge yourself to grow, if you want to increase your confidence and beauty – inside and out - and join a supportive group of women, I highly recommend finding a pageant in your area and going for it! (oooorrrrr even just reaching out to a local pageant woman near you and grabbing coffee). Joining a pageant was one of the best decisions I made. I have no doubt you will be greatly surprised at how positively it affects your life. #morethanaprettyface).

Anyways, back to the story about my "friend..." After seeing how I had been even more involved in the community, she started to volunteer at an organization I had been involved in because she was inspired by my work in the community. And I thought that was *great*! If my contribution could inspire someone else to get more involved in their community, don't we all win?! (or so I thought...).

My "friend" was so excited for me when I unexpectedly won the entire pageant competition and became the State Titleholder. She said she was my biggest fan and *knew* it would be me. She was proud of me, proud to be my friend, and happy to stand by my side. She knew me, who I was, she knew my heart, my hopes and dreams and that they were coming from a good place. She knew my intention was to use the influence of the Title for good...to work with other non-profit organizations, to speak to kids, to work with the underserved...*that's* what it was all about and what my intention was the entire time.

My "friend" and I had been each other's "person" for the last ten years, and we had been through a lot. We were by each other's side through thick and thin, through finding love, losing love, through business ventures, the girls' nights and the BFF necklaces. We shared our hopes and dreams with each other, had each other's backs, stayed up way too late talking about "all the things" and always had a lot of fun together. We stood next to each other at our weddings, as each of us promised our hearts to our husbands. She was my bestie and my "sister from another mister" (as we would say).

And now this? A public blast of me and "who I had become?" Apparently, according to her, I had "totally changed in the span of a weekend of a competition." (insert palm to the face move again). In her words, I was a narcissist, I was selfish, I didn't deserve to win, that pageants were nothing but insecure women vying for the stage and for attention... And *she would never..."*

I was so confused. I felt betrayed. Misunderstood. Hurt. Wasn't she supposed to be happy for me?

Then...it magnified. The toxin of gossip and tearing someone (me) down spread like wildfire. She got together with a few of my other "friends" and unloaded more ammo. Hurtful words. Slander. Name-calling. Backstabbing. It seemed to be a social-media and a gossip-sesh frenzy. Hurtful comments bred more hurtful comments and likes and shares. #unfriended.

Isn't it interesting how quickly something so negative can grow? Isn't it interesting how someone can be a friend, but then the moment you try and do something new, they tear you down for it? I've talked to countless women who have been in similar situations. Whether they started a new business, changed careers, or started to voice their truth, some of their closest friends were the first ones to take a stab at them.

This very thing can actually be found in nature, besides just the human race. It's called "the crab-mentality." If you put crabs in a pot or a bucket, and if one tries to climb out, the other crabs will try and pull it down. If that same crab continues to try to climb out, the other crabs will literally break its legs off or even attempt to kill the crab. (see the video in this chapter's resources at **CharityMajors.com/MeantForMore**).

I felt like the crab being pulled back down. My heart was crushed. I was hurt. I felt humiliated. I felt attacked - like 100 arrows had been shot right through me. The logical side of my brain said this was a stupid situation. #firstworldproblems And I should just suck it up and move on…that I didn't need her anyways. But my heart didn't understand. I couldn't see where the disconnect was from being encouraged and supported a few weeks earlier to being publicly shamed by my best friend of ten years.

I wondered, how was I "here" again? I thought this childish stuff was behind me. Weren't we past high school and college? You see, this wasn't the first time this had happened. That's the thing about repeating patterns that show up in your life…they will continue to show up so that you can learn the lesson to a greater depth.

There have been other instances in my life where someone has verbally slandered me. Remember the saying, "Sticks and stones will break my bones, but words will never hurt me?" Well, bull-crap to that! Words (the wrong words), are one of the most hurtful things in the world. I have felt the pain over and over, all throughout my life. This was one of my life patterns. Although I was raised in a supportive and encouraging family, I still experienced hurt by people who were either role models in my life or people I was close to and knew my heart, my hopes, my dreams, my flaws, quirks, and were there on good days and bad days. That's why it hurt so bad...these people were "my people" (or so I thought...).

Because I had been told by a coach that he didn't like my personality, I would never play in a volleyball match, I took on the belief that there was something wrong with who I was on the inside. I am a first born, so my natural leadership qualities were deemed as being bossy. I was teased in high school for being in the National Honor Society, so I felt stupid for being smart. Some guys told me I was "too pretty" for them or that I was "intimidating" so the sting of rejection for how I was made, *dug deep*. Being a tall but somewhat shy high school girl earned me the title of a B@%$& among other girls. Wearing a ribbon in my hair, while I dominated on the volleyball court, made me too girly for the sporty girls, but being a high-level athlete made me too sporty for the girly girls. I was even hazed and called horrible names by fellow teammates because I stood my ground and wouldn't shot gun a beer at an initiating hazing party. My positive attitude and ability to see the best in others or in a situation has prompted others to tell me that I live in "Positivity La-La Land" and ride on a magical unicorn and they would rather live in their reality than be near me.

I constantly felt like how I was made was a mistake and that I didn't belong.

This is where the shame of my unique design, a smart, a positive, natural leader, pretty, and outgoing girl who loved people began. This is where the things that God had given me, became curses rather than gifts. And when I say, "unique design," I mean the unique combination of personality, strengths, gifts, and looks that God gives someone. *You* have a unique divine design too. A beautiful combination that only *you* have. A unique design and purpose that only *you* can fulfill because of the combination of gifts that you have been given. You are a walking God-dream that was imagined in the heart of God, He put flesh on you and knew you would be exactly what the world needed at this exact time in all of eternity.

The part that we all go through is the attack on who we are and the beautiful potential of the call that lies within us to make the world a better place and more like heaven. I used to think that my looks, my natural gifts of leadership, being smart, and always seeing the best in others – the way God made me – was a mistake. Have you ever felt that way? Like the things you love, the things you are naturally good at are the very things that cause someone else to try and tear you down?

I was tired of other women looking me up and down and giving me the stink eye. I was tired of being too "intimidating" for a guy and feeling the pain of rejection. As a people lover, I just wanted relationship – real connections with people who didn't pre-judge me and knew and loved me for *me*. Because of this desire, but due to the negative feedback I was receiving from the outside world, I began to "dim my light" (as I like to call it). I began to downplay my beauty, dress in sweats, and I tried a lot of different hair styles and colors that did not bring out the best in me. I hid behind an extra 20 pounds and quieted my people-loving personality. I started to play small. I hid in the background crippled by fear of rejection.

I dimmed my light so that others wouldn't feel inferior or self-conscious around me anymore. I became quiet. I put up walls. I wore masks to hide the real me. I became an achiever, a do-er, and a people pleaser. I could achieve my way to the top with the best of them because if I was too busy achieving something, I didn't have to be real enough to be hurt by others. I had more masks than a girl has shoes. I was striving to do it all and make it look easy. I tried to keep it together, make it look perfect, keep straight A's, and have my hair, nails, clothes, and makeup look just right. But if that was "too much" for some people, on went the sweat pants again. And don't forget the "don't let them see you sweat" (or fart) part of it. It...was...*exhausting*...

Now, don't get me wrong, things like makeup, fashion, and the desire to look and feel confident on the outside is a good thing. I've always thought that. There are actions we can do that enhance what we are naturally given and to bring out our God-given beauty. We can put on makeup, do our hair, wear fashionable clothes and push-up bras (all the mamas know a good push-up bra and some lip gloss is helpful for confidence and feeling more put together). I love a good lipstick and pair of pants that make my butt look good. Those physical actions of enhancing beauty have been a part of human civilization from the beginning of time. Even Cleopatra wore eyeliner and lipstick, jewelry and beautiful garments. And those actions – in balance to accentuate what is already there – are not wrong.

But it's when we use these actions of external beauty to *hide* who we really are, or compensate for where we feel we're lacing, well, that's where the shame is found. Shame is hiding behind *layers* of makeup that is caked on so that no one can see your freckles because you hate them (hiding who you are and how you were made). And yes, I used to do this.

Shame is either hiding in clothes (or behind your kids) because you are ashamed of your body and how it looks. Or the opposite of that, which is over-flaunting your assets because you have been taught that is how you get positive interaction and attention with people. So, you mask your personality with over-exposure of your physical assets, almost to draw attention away from who you are and just show what you have. And yes, I used to do this, too.

I know what it's like to feel foolish, believing who I was wasn't good enough, smart enough, pretty enough... Or at times I was too much for someone - too pretty, too smart, or too tall. My beliefs, the things that made me, me, were criticized and made me feel like who I was and how I was created, was *all wrong*. Gosh, do I know that feeling all too well.

I can't say that I've felt the pain of physical abuse or sexual abuse and the shame that comes along with that, so please understand that I am not downplaying those injustices.

These are definitely a part of the attempt that comes to try and knock a person off track instead of using the trials to fulfill their purpose.

I can say that movements like the recent social media movement of #metoo, shed light on a lot of darkness about physical and sexual abuse, that has been hiding for far too long.

I believe there has been a step towards understanding, freedom, and healing due to sharing those stories. What I can share from personal experience, (and because it's in one of my favorite books that I base my life on), is that I believe there is *life and death in the power of the tongue* and what is said either speaks life and light, or death and destruction.

And here's the thing...*we* get to *choose* which words we believe.

Even as I write this, my internal monologue, my ego (or what I like to call my "inner-critic) is trying to get me to feel humiliation and foolish - to shame me because these "little wounds" aren't as "big" as physical or sexual abuse...My ego tells me my wounds are:

*"#firstworldproblems"*

*"These wounds you experience aren't worth talking about."*

*"They won't care about your story or your message because you are the only one who feels that way."*

*"No one will listen or care."*

*"There are bigger problems to worry about like starving kids in Africa."*

*"Who are you to say this kind of stuff?"*

*"You're nobody."*

*"You're not a writer or a psychologist or an expert in any of this."*

*"You're not smart enough to talk about this."*

*"Who you are is not enough."*

Well, isn't that fun to listen to? #insertwideeyesemoji. The thing about shame is that it comes at us from multiple angles. According to Webster, it can come from others who use shame as a verb or action – "(of a person, action, or situation) make (someone) feel ashamed." Shame can also come from ourselves… from the internal dialogue that resides deep down in our subconscious, that we have somehow attached a belief to an action from somewhere in our past.

Now, there is a difference between shame and guilt, and I believe it's important to know the difference. Shame is "I *am* bad," while guilt is "I *did something* bad." Guilt is "I *made a* mistake". Shame is "I *AM* a mistake". See the difference? Guilt is about the action while shame is about the person – the being.

In her book, *The Shameless Life: Recognize Your Shame and Overcome It*, Terilee Harrison shares the power in shame isn't what happened to you or what you have done, the power in shame is in what you *think*.

## Shame comes from 3 places:

You can feel shame about how you're made. Shame is personal. What you feel intense shame about may be "no big deal" to someone else. You can be you're too tall, too short, too fat, too thin, your skin is too light, your skin is too dark, you're too smart, or you're not smart enough. The list is endless.

You can feel shame from the things others have done to you. A third of the humans walking this planet have been physically abused by others. This is NOT okay. At a minimum, you may have had someone say hurtful words which have stuck with you and caused you to feel shame.

You can feel shame from your mistakes. We all have done things we are not proud of. But sometimes you can feel more than guilt about what you've done, you can come to believe that *you* are bad.

In Terilee's case, she was born with an underdeveloped reproductive tract and came to believe when she was 12 years old that she was different from *all* other girls. Although she looked pretty on the outside, for years she felt ugly on the inside. No one would have guessed how much she didn't like herself. The thing is, what you believe on the inside is what you will manifest on the outside. She felt so unlovable she began to make all kinds of bad decisions in her life. Her low vibes just attracted more low vibes in her life. Thankfully things have changed for her and she is now reaching out to help others overcome their shame.

I believe that bringing *every wound*, big and little, to light, as insignificant or as #firstworldproblem-y as it may sound to you or me or our (mainly *my*) internal monologue. *All of it* needs to be brought to light. We can only find things in the dark when we shed light on them, so here I am, flashlight in hand (well, more like a big spotlight – which feels bright and harsh and vulnerable) shining a light on all of my "junk", on my wounds, fears, and insecurities, I'm hoping to give you permission to begin to shine a light on yours, too, so that we can *all* move toward the path of healing and wholeness. I'm also shining a light on these things because I don't believe I am the only one that feels this way. There is power in #metoo.

I believe other women bury their feelings of not being good enough, being too perfect, being intimidating or bossy because it isn't a "big enough wound" to talk about. Guess what, Girlfriend? #ifeelyou and #itmatters. I know what it's like to bury the feeling of not being good enough or being too much or being not pretty enough or being too pretty. I know how you feel when someone says that you are intimidating or bossy or they put you in the category of a shallow dumb blonde and a pretty person with no depth or substance to them because that's just how #prettypeople are - shallow, with no substance.

Here's the thing about wounds... They hurt regardless of the size. Whether you get a splinter in your hand or it is cut with a knife, it still hurts. I sometimes think the small splinter-wounds that go unseen by the naked eye are even more painful than the trauma of a large wound. Because they fester, (and usually multiple splinters get layered on top of each other), they are below the surface, buried in the swampland of shame, and they dig a little deeper with each movement. They can cause serious infection if not dealt with.

It seems like there is more "grace," forgiveness or understanding for a "knife-size" wound... like, "oh, she was in an abusive relationship so that's why..." or "yea, she was sexually abused when she was younger, so we can let her actions slide..." You can visibly see the wound and scar and so somehow that makes people understand or accept it more.

Or at least this has been my experience. I've known people that struggle with horrible addiction due to the experiences of abuse they have had from their past. Because of this hurt and unhealed wound, they have lashed out in destructive ways that have hurt a lot of people, torn families apart, and destroyed careers. And I've seen it happen time and time again, the excuses that were made for their destructive behavior, were because of the unresolved trauma that occurred.

I'm not saying I don't have compassion for these people. My heart truly goes out to them in hopes that they begin to seek the healing they need and own the truth and the power of what could be their story...it just seems like there are more egg shells that are walked on, more things that are hidden, and more excuses made for major trauma when in reality, all hurting hearts matter.

And yet, on the other hand, I've known other people who refused to become the victim and have turned horrible situations around in an incredible way that leads the way for the healing of thousands of lives. I guess the point is, is that *we get to choose* how our story evolves…we *get to* take our power back…we get to draw on the strength we have gained from the hardest of times and *choose* to use them for good instead of staying in a place of victimhood and lashing out on others.

And let's go back to the "splinter" size wounds – the ones that sound like "#prettypeopleproblems," #firstworldproblems or "oh you're beautiful, so you don't have any problems," or "you're too perfect," or "gosh, wouldn't it be nice to be you…" Splinters. Our egos (and other people) like to tell us that they don't matter. The splinters that dig deeper and deeper. Splinters that get stacked upon more splinters. Wounds that fester and hurt.

They…matter…too…but they can *no longer be an excuse.*

So yes, Beautiful One, whether or not you have experienced splinter size wounds or knife-size wounds, they still hurt. Whether you have experienced 100 hurtful comments about your appearance or about who you are, one traumatic experience such as rape or abuse or loss, it still hurts. Your 100 splinters are still painful. So are mine. Your big wound is still painful. So is mine. And I'm here to validate them. *All of them.* The big and the little. To say that you are not alone, and that your splinters and holes *do matter.*

Especially the splinters. They matter because they can lead to bigger habits of self-destruction. They actually matter a lot. And it matters that we do a little digging to uproot them, so we can heal, because the magic is found in the healing process. When you are brave enough to venture through the swamp of shame and start your healing process, you give others permission to be brave and seek healing in their lives, too.

Shame is highly correlated with addiction, depression, violence, bullying, eating disorders, obesity, aggression, control, and suicide. Can you think back to times where you have felt any of these negative side effects? Ways that bring you away from truly loving and accepting yourself? Can you follow the rabbit trail even farther and think of where these actions stem from? Think of every time you acted out in a way that stemmed from the deeper issue of shame. Think of the ways you acted in a way that you didn't love yourself...most of these actions can lead back to an emotional attachment to a limiting belief that is rooted in shame.

For example, if you have dealt with an eating disorder, there may be certain points throughout your life that triggered your beliefs about food and your body or how a void was filled or you numbed pain with food. These beliefs took hold sometime in your past – usually childhood.

This is called the "root" of the problem or *"root cause."*

But there's good news... You can change the way you take on that belief. You just have to do the work and the uprooting that comes with it and invite God to give you His perspective. You have the power to go back to the origin of the belief (big or small), detach from that belief, and attach a new, positive belief. In the Christian world, we call this SOZO and it's a really powerful and healing experience. One I highly recommend.

Healing is a process, it takes time, and it never fully goes away, wounds turn to scars, but the emotional charge can dissipate and you can build up a "shame resistance", as Brene Brown likes to call it. For example, when someone used to say something negative about me, I would be devastated. It would hurt me to the core of who I was and send me into a negative tailspin. My head would flood with a frenzy of hurtful thoughts and words, and I would isolate myself.

Over time, I learned healing techniques to detach from the initial belief I attached to my subconscious. I then learned ways to reframe the story and attach new positive beliefs to those same life events. I invited the voice of Truth - the One that created me - to speak identity over me. Once I started doing this, I began to heal, grow and believe in who (and who's) I was. I became more confident in how my Creator made me and negative comments didn't hurt as much. I started to believe that everything was happening *for* me and that God was working everything out for my good. Negativity started to bounce off the armor of my self-worth and the belief that I am not a mistake, that God made me just the way He intended to, that I am enough, I have what it takes, and that I am here for #justatimeasthis. I started listening to a different conversation in my head.

That I was *#MeantforMore*.

You, too, can build up your armor, but you must first dig out the splinters. The healing of these shame splinters starts with knowing yourself at a deeper level and loving and accepting who you are and how God made you, who He calls you despite what anyone else says or thinks because, let's face it, they are dealing with their own wounds, too.

It comes down to believing that your unique design is *not a mistake*. Your *too much* is not a mistake. You are here for such a time as this. You *are* smart enough, good enough, and you have what it takes. You *are* worthy, you *are* loved, and you *are* perfect just the way you are – flaws and all. You are perfectly imperfect. It comes with the strength in knowing that everything from your past has a lesson you can learn, that it happened *for* you, to show you the strength you have inside, and that you are here *on purpose for a purpose.*

When you can operate from a space of trust and belief in those words of Truth, it will reflect in your actions and how you show up in the world. For me, I no longer hide in sweat pants, and I am at home in my beauty, in my leadership, in my love of nerding out on books, and in the fact that I like pretty things. I like floral prints, flowy-fabrics, pinks and golds, and sparkly things. I'm bold and feminine. I'm strong and gentle. I'm brave and vulnerable. I'm beautiful and kind. I can hold two truths at the same time.

I no longer worry that if I wear those things someone is going to say, "I'm too girly" or "I'm prissy" or "too pretty" because I also know that I've got this Zena-Princess-Warrior/Wonder Woman mixed with a Disney Princess vibe and under my pretty floral dress is a big, awesome sword that can chop the Devil's head off.

Another thing I've learned is to be very intentional about who I have now surrounded myself with. (Remember those mirror neurons? It matters *who* you surround yourself with)... I believe that there are women out there, like me, who believe that we, as women, are meant to live in sisterhood. To live in harmony, grace, support, and love for each other instead of insecure competition that tears down one another. We have a desire to be the rising tide that raises all ships, not the crabs in the bucket that tear each other down.

The bottom line to all of this stuff, is living what Author and founder of the Bliss Project, Lori Harder, likes to call the "F-it" life. In her book, A Tribe Called Bliss, she talks about "F-ing" them in the car, on the street, in your bed, in the kitchen, all over town. And the F-word she is talking about is *Forgiveness*. Forgiving everyone, everywhere, at every chance you get. (and this includes yourself).

Here's the thing about forgiveness...it's meant to give freedom to the person giving the forgiveness, not the other way around. I used to stay so stuck in my pride and not offer forgiveness to others that hurt me. But the thing is, it's like drinking poison and expecting the other person to die. Holding onto un-forgiveness is something that literally hurts ourselves.

Offering forgiveness doesn't mean you agree with the other person's actions. It means that you are willing to release the hold their actions have had on you. This is where we gain our power back and get to *choose another response.* No...Matter...What...

I invite you to offer forgiveness, over and over, to anyone and everyone who has ever hurt you...and this includes yourself as well as those that you thought were "your people."

Through the healing of forgiveness I've found, I am able to look back at the past friendship I had with the girl that I mentioned at the beginning of the chapter, and *I am grateful for it.* Through the gaining and losing of that friendship, I learned *so much*. I learned who I want to surround myself with. I've learned what *not* to do and how *not* to treat others. I learned about the masks that I had up that kept me guarded and inauthentic and how that contributed to the toxic friendship that it was. I've learned that there is a gift in everything. I've learned more about perception and how people view others based on the wounds they have received from their past. I've learned how to love and accept someone with compassion for what they may be going through and how to pray for them, even when they hurt me. And from the things I've learned, I truly and wholeheartedly hope and pray that she is doing well, loving life and letting her own light shine.

My guess is that you have a similar vibe as me – that Wonder Woman / Zena-Princess-Warrior / Disney Princess / sisterhood vibe - because "like attracts like" and you wouldn't be reading this book if you didn't have it. My guess is that you, like me, are also here *for such a time* as this and you have known this, deep down in your heart, for your entire life.

You believe that there is more in store for you...and it's #BIG. Bigger than you may know or care to believe, but there is an inner knowing (whether you like to admit it or not) that tells you that you are here for a special reason. I believe it, and I invite you to begin to believe it, too.

*#WeARE*Meant*forMore*

I also invite you to dive into more resources that can empower you to build your shame resilience, own your God given beauty, to forgive and build your body armor at **www.CharityMajors.com/MeantForMore**. You can find the resources under this chapter in the Resources section.

Chapter 5

# Package That Matches the Contents

> "Elegance is when the inside is as beautiful as the outside."
>
> -Coco Chanel

#WeAreMeantForMore
@CharityMajors

# Chapter 5

# Package That Matches the Contents

Now that we've journeyed through some of the swampland and understand that you don't have to hide who you are in shame anymore, there are ways that you can accentuate your assets and have the outside match the inside.

So slip those mud boots off friend...it's time to learn about the fun stuff!

This is the part where my beauty queen experience comes into play because I think beauty doesn't have to be just on the inside or just on the outside. I believe it is meant to be *both*.

Before we dive into the resources and concepts, I'm curious as to whether or not you have ever gotten a drink and thought it was one thing and when you took a sip, it was something completely different? How did you feel? It catches you off guard, right? It is surprising, kind of puzzling and sometimes causes liquid to come out of your nostrils. #thatmayormaynothavehappenedtome

Maybe you've experienced this because you are a Coke fan but you were given a Pepsi, and you were just downright pissed. (I've heard this is a very serious offense!) (Side note—I am not endorsing drinking soda of any kind...it's bad for you. Seriously though... Stop drinking soda. Remember the chapter about doing things to support your body and the call on your life? Soda does not do that. Your insides will thank me later. #steppingoff-soapbox).

The way that you dress, do your makeup, your hairstyle and types of jewelry can create the same effects as the wrong drink— the confusion, the being puzzled, the liquid coming out of nostrils #okaymaybenotthatone - if you don't "wrap yourself" in a way that matches who you are on the inside.

Let me explain... Remember how your subconscious picks up on over 80,000 signals at any given moment? Parts of the signals that get picked up happen to be with your appearance. Remember how we are naturally attracted to things of symmetry, and things that appear "healthy?" This is an innate thing that got passed down from our cavemen ancestors and it's a little concept called "the strong survive". We subconsciously pick up on signals like healthy, glowing skin, thick hair, good posture, muscle tone, and healthy teeth because these things are a window into how healthy our body is on the inside, how able we are to reproduce and keep a species alive.

Besides just keeping a species alive, implementing these concepts within our businesses is also proven to be *very* helpful. Another online marketing entrepreneur friend of mine did a study when he was doing his high ticket video sales calls. For the sales video calls that he did in his professional looking studio, dressed up nicely and looking the part of the professional that he is, he closed *double* the sales, compared to the video sales calls that he did when he was in his home wearing a t-shirt. The setting and background of the video call, along with what he was wearing made a big difference! (thousands and thousands of dollars of a difference).

I've also experienced similar results. When I was a personal trainer, I would go to networking meetings in between clients. Sometimes I would stay in my "trainer attire," consisting of super cute workout clothes and other times I would wear a cute blouse, nice jeans or slacks and some high heels. The quality of connections I made were always better when I was dressed nicer. More of my ideal clients showed up to purchase training from me when I looked more professional. I had the opportunity to train and coach some of the most influential people in my community because when I realized this concept, I owned it and began to attract my ideal clients.

I'm not saying there isn't ever a place for "athleisure wear," a messy bun, or that you need to be dressed to the nine's at all moments of every day. I'm suggesting that if you are wanting to grow your business, increase your influence, build your brand, connect with other high level people in the community, serve more people, sell more programs, or whatever it may be that you are meant for, there is value in honoring your appearance and showing up put together.

So, as you can see, not only does having healthy skin, hair, nails, and complexion matter, but so does the way we "package" our body. Did you know that there are certain colors, shapes, and fabrics that best fit different personalities? It's true! Think back about the drink analogy...or here's another one to let your brain wrap around this concept. If you had a bag of potato chips, reached in, and it was cheese puffs, you would be a little puzzled, right? (I'm not sure why these analogies are using junk food...I don't even eat potato chips or cheese puffs...but whatever...you get the point. Now go eat an apple and drink some Kombucha). #formerhealthcoach #icanthelpit #LOL Anyway... You would be puzzled because what was on the inside didn't match the package, right?

YOU are the same way! You have a certain personality and it shows up in your facial features; in the way you express your emotions, how you speak, your expressions, your body language, your posture, your energy, the confidence you show when you wear certain things, etc. And if you are wearing the wrong colors, textiles, fabrics, cuts of clothing, shapes of jewelry, the wrong haircut or color, or something that you don't feel as confident in, all this stuff creates incongruency with how others interpret who you really are.

Insert subconscious signals being picked up from someone else – if you wear a color that clashes with your personality, it creates a subconscious signal that the other person picks up that you aren't who you say you are. There is also a deeper subconscious energy that you will have because you may not feel as confident in what you are wearing or how you are presenting yourself because it feels incongruent – it feels "off."

Have you ever seen a shirt or outfit – either on Pinterest, on a friend or on a hanger – and it looked awesome?! You just had to buy it right away?! You bring it home, try it on, expecting to feel as awesome as it looked on that random girl on Instagram, but when you put it on, it doesn't give you the same feeling? That's because it may not be something that fits you and your "being." But here's the catch (I know because I used to do this all the time) – what do we do with this piece of clothing? We keep it – with the tags still on – and hang it in our closet and tell yourself that we will try it on again another day. Maybe it's just a "fat day" or our hair is off.

Then what happens? A week later, we try it on again, when we are having a really good hair day and still, it makes us feel "blah." We can't seem to get rid of it because of how cute it looked on someone else, so it stays in our closet, with hopes that one day, it will recreate that feeling we had when we saw it on Pinterest, but it goes unworn in our closet and takes up space. And now our closet is overstuffed with clothes that don't bring that feeling of #yeeaaahhguuurrrllll when we put it on, we have a hard time deciding on what to wear because most of it doesn't make us feel great, and our self-confidence goes down.

Sound familiar? Have you ever experienced this? I didn't know that when I was doing this, it traced back to having a closet full of stuff that didn't match my "being." I didn't know there was a way to dress so that it best suited me, my personality, my facial features, and how I wanted to show up in the world (and that when this concept is understood, it could *save me money and space in my closet*).

You might be thinking, well gosh, this sounds really complicated. I just want to go to the store and pick something out without having to analyze the color, shape, cut, textile and fabric type. I am here to reassure you that once you know your "type" and have guidelines to follow, shopping becomes easier and more enjoyable. It is easier to let go of the clothes that are taking up space in your closet that you hope to wear one day.

It makes it easy to pick out things that best suit who you really are and how you want to show up in the world. Your confidence will drastically increase. Your closet will be less cluttered. You will save time when you pick out outfits, you will save money because you aren't wasting it on buying things that sit in your closet and never get worn. You will be sending off subconscious signals that you are in integrity with who you are. Your package will match the contents. There will be no ugly weird subconscious signaling to your beautiful self.

This concept comes from a great book called "It's Just My Nature," by Carol Tuttle. I definitely recommend reading it. Once you get this concept, it changes everything!

No more awkward spitting out the wrong drink. No more liquid coming out of nostrils or frowning in puzzlement because you pulled out a different chip from the bag. Just the right message at the right time, in integrity with who you are and how you were made. Which is perfect and beautiful. *And for such a time as this...*

I invite you to not only grab a copy of Carol's book, but to take some time and go through your closet. Sort through the things that you have and if it doesn't "spark joy," as my good friend and author of *Purple Crayon Confidence*, Kayla-Leah Rich, likes to say, then get rid of it.

How do you know if something "sparks joy?" It's that outfit or piece of clothing or pair of shoes that when you wear it, you feel like a million bucks and nothing could wreck your mojo. It makes you feel giddy inside, not "blah." Put it on, feel all the feels, and then as you try on other articles of clothing from your closet, if it doesn't give you those same feelings, out it goes!

With clothes that no longer spark joy, I like to suggest "thanking them" for serving their purpose in your life and donating them so they can serve those in need. And if you need the cash to get other articles of clothing that make you feel like a million bucks, then by all means, sell the "non-joy-sparking items" and go shopping with the cash.

Before you go shopping, or if you are struggling to find which type of clothing best fits you, I want to invite you to take a FREE Energy Profile Assessment on my website. This energy profile assessment will give you an idea of how you were made and which energy matches what fabrics, shapes, colors, textiles, etc. If you want to dive deeper and take the actual course (which is one of my favorites), there is also a discount code so that you can match your contents with your package. Visit **CharityMajors.com/MeantForMore** and find the tab for this chapter.

Chapter 6

# Monkey Bars vs. Selfie Sticks

> "When you come to the end of all light that you know and are about to drop off into the darkness of the unknown, faith is knowing that one of two things will happen: There will be something solid to stand on or you will be taught to fly."
>
> -Unknown
>
> #WeAreMeantForMore
> @CharityMajors

**Chapter 6**

## Monkey Bars vs. Selfie Sticks

I remember it vividly. I was hanging there, legs dangling in the air, my knuckles were turning white, my hands were starting to burn, and the ground was a long way off. "Daddy, but will you really catch me if I let go?" I squealed. "Yes, Love Bug, I will catch you. Even though you can't see me, I'm here, and I won't let you fall."

I was about 5 years old, and my dad and I were at a playground. I had been running around like the carefree happy child that I was (probably dreaming about being in happy la-la land riding my unicorn, or maybe I was a Disney Princess with my super cool warrior sword). I decided today was the day I would go all the way across the big kid monkey bars. One rung after the other, I started to make my way across what seemed to be the longest monkey bar set known to my 5-year-old self, but my tired, little hands and fingers could barely hang on for another second.

My dad was close by, he heard me calling for him, and he came over. Being the wise man that he is, he chose to use this little playground as a teaching moment. He stood behind me and told me he would catch me if I fell. I couldn't see him, but I could hear him. "I won't let you fall. I promise. You can trust me." I held on tighter, wiggling in fear, and still questioning if my dad would actually catch me or whether I would end up in a full body cast because every bone in my little body would be shattered the moment I hit the ground that was so far away. "Even though you can't see me, trust that I am right here. You can hear my voice. Let go. I won't let you fall."

I couldn't tell if I had mustered up enough bravery to actually let go or if my tired, little hands finally gave out, but I eventually squeezed my eyes shut and let go. I let go, and I somehow just *knew*, and I fell right into my dad's loving arms, just like he promised.

That day, a life lesson was etched into my little heart. One that I will never forget, and one that I believe shapes who I am today. I learned about *trust*. I learned to trust not only my dad, but I learned to trust the voice of Truth that lived inside of me. The voice that spoke to my heart and called me, Beloved. The voice that never condemned me but drew me to a higher standard of myself and called out the best in me. The voice that was typically deeper and quieter than the other chattering voices that I hear in my head, but it was the voice I trusted the most. It is the voice of God.

Wayne Dyer says, "When we learn to trust ourselves, we learn to trust the very wisdom that created us." Don't you just love that?

But here's the thing about learning to trust our intuition and that voice of truth…it's not always as easy as it sounds. Most people stop listening to that "still small voice" because there is either too much noise coming from their inner critic or outside sources, or they don't trust their intuition because when they did, the situation ended up blowing up in their face. Or maybe they trusted the voice of God and the situation ended up not looking like anything they thought.

Here's the thing about learning to trust your intuition and the voice of God. It takes practice and it takes the understanding that, even if you make a decision where you trust your inner knowing and it seems like things around you fall apart or that you may not like it, that it's happening *exactly* how it should for...your...good...

Our Creator *knows exactly* what we need, even before we do. It's like when I know that my son is tired and needs a nap. He may not think he is tired or that he needs some rest, so he may give his best protest, or give me the cutest puppy dog eyes and asks to stay awake, but as his mom, I know that he needs that nap and that's what's best for him in that moment, even if he doesn't understand.

Learning to trust our inner wisdom and the voice of God is kind of like that. It's trusting that as we take bold and inspired action because of the truth that we are choosing to believe in, even if it's the harder decision, even if we don't know how it's going to turn out, we *trust* that everything is happening FOR us, and will all be worked out *for our good*.

Besides learning the art of trust, we also must be mindful of the "noise." There was a time in my life where I began to ignore this inner voice because of all of the noise around me. I began to shut it out and listen to so many other things. I began to listen to the other kids who would make fun of me or pick me last. I began to listen to the coach who told me he didn't like my personality. I began to listen to the voice of the boy who rejected me. The message from the media that said I wasn't pretty enough, perfect enough, or airbrushed enough. I began to listen to the voice of society that said I should just hunker down, find a good job, work for 40 hours a week for the next 40 years, be a good girl, go to church, act like I'm happy and like everything is okay and live in a perfect little house with my perfect little family and cook perfect little dinners. I began to listen to all of the social media chatter that never seemed to slow down or shut up. The posts, the comments, the filters, the best parts of everyone's day, while all I felt like was a failure, not good enough, not pretty enough, not smart enough, and I kept dimming the places where I was "too much" so I wouldn't offend anyone.

The noise of all of the other voices around me had drowned out the still small voice of truth inside of me.

I have a feeling I'm not the only one who has experienced too much noise. How does this happen? How have we, as a society, slipped into this mindless existence of never ending chatter, constant scrolling down the social media feed, feeling numb, being busy but not being effective, wasting time, and not living the life we are truly called to live? How do we find our way out of this norm that keeps our "meant for more-ness" staying "less than"?

Well, we keep going back to the "too much noise" (especially from social media) because it's…science…

Studies show that social media gives the same dopamine response as alcohol, smoking, and gambling. Dopamine is the neurotransmitter that signals to the brain a positive response. Epinephrine does the same thing but there is a difference. Dopamine is short lived while epinephrine is a "slower burning" response. It's kind of like a camp fire… Dopamine is the kindling while epinephrine is the log. The log might take a little more to actually catch fire and get hot, but when it does, it burns a lot longer than the kindling and it has a higher function – to put out heat.

Dopamine and Epinephrine work the same way in the brain… Dopamine is meant to only be the kindling when it comes to "igniting" happiness in our brain and Epinephrine is meant to be the longer sustaining sensation of fulfillment, love, and connection. But what happens when, in today's world, most of the love and connection that we are chasing is fueled by the kindling – the superficial connection and rush of Dopamine that we feel when we look at our social media… when I get more likes on a post, when we get good comments on that last selfie we took. When someone shares a good quote that I made up in a new app that I found that has the coolest font and I watermarked it with my @handle?

It makes us feel good. It makes us feel popular, liked and significant, right? But *only with kindling*. Only with the superficial shot of neurotransmitters that burn off quickly, so we search for more. We search for another hit. Another viral post. Another post in the perfect selfie position with an even better filter so that it will get even more likes this time because my duck face was even better.

What's wrong with us? Well…nothing. We are hard-wired to move towards pleasure and away from pain so when we feel the Dopamine hit of "approval and likes and significance and shares and acceptance" from our "friends" and "followers" (as social media has so conveniently labeled them), it fulfills a deeper need that we, as humans, instinctually have and need to survive. The need for connection. The need for love and belonging. The need to feel accepted, significant, and that we are making a difference in someone's life. #Pleasure

I'll be honest when I say that I am concerned for the younger generations who have grown up with a phone in their hand and a digital friends list that they seek approval from. Over half of teenagers reported having been bullied over social media. One out of ten adolescents and teens have reported that they have had an embarrassing photo taken of them, unknowingly, and it was posted without their knowledge or consent. (3)

And with access to social celebrities who are seeking attention in an unhealthy way and using their influence simply for likes and comments on their duck face photos and revealing breast or booty photos, what type of messaging is the world sending back to these younger generations? I believe it is creating such an unsafe, disconnected, not-accepting, have-to-be-perfect and superficial understanding of the world around these children, at a deep subconscious level.

I only *hope* that we, as parents/adults/those who have learned a little along the way, have been able to heal our hearts enough to provide them with the depth and the relationship and acceptance and the teachings that failure is a part of life, enough to equip them for this crazy digital world and where it's headed.

When it comes to social media, I believe the problem is that we aren't getting the deeper connection that we need to thrive and to actually be fulfilled and satisfied. It's all kindling. We don't have the deeper conversations with a person face to face, because it's way easier to shoot out a general message in between errands throughout our busy day. It's easier to type out a mean response to a screen and push send than it is to say it to an actual person. We don't have conflict resolution skills because all we do is delete and block someone out of our lives instead of sit face to face, cry, share our hearts, seek to understand their side of the story, listen, validate, share how we really feel, how we hurt, and offer and receive forgiveness. We only see the perfection, and never the failures. We only see the good times and not the bad.

Empathy is at an all-time low because we see our friend's kid, a cat video, our aunt's sandwich that she ate for lunch, and a starving child in Africa, all within the same scroll of a finger. We measure our life to Pinterest and the perfect blog photos that we save and pin, hoping that we can clean our kitchen enough to take a decent photo to post. We've lost the ability to truly connect in a world that has never been more connected.

Now don't get me wrong. I'm not saying burn your phone, never get on social media again, move to the mountains, never shower, grow a beard, and live off the land. Shower for God's sake. #showeringisgood Social media can be a great tool to stay in contact with family and friends, to share a message, to support a business, to meet someone from a different part of the world, to raise awareness for charitable organizations, etc. It's also a great place to find a super supportive tribe in a Facebook group, like ours. #shamelessplug

But when it comes to social media, how much is too much, how far is too far, how much noise is too much noise, and how many mindless scrolls with our fingers are too many scrolls? When is the comparison we naturally and constantly do with everyone else's highlight reel and our everyday messy lives enough? When do we stop hiding behind a screen and truly connect with someone, soul to soul? How much of this dark side of what can be a great tool are we going to stand for? How do we get back to the innocent place of hanging from the monkey bars, falling into a loving community, and trusting the voice inside of us instead of the other voices that are bombarding us from every angle?

I believe the answer to this comes by healing our hearts first and finding the true connection – the log that burns big and bright, over the kindling – connecting soul to soul, heart to heart, human to human, within a tribe and community that lifts you up and encourages your fire to shine bright.

Use social media to find someone that has a similar mission to you, and then create, foster, and nurture that connection in real life. Follow the right role models and influencers – the ones that are using their influence to **impact people and not just impress them**. Create a beautiful space in your home that *you* love, vs. what Pinterest or a blogger says to love.

Be intentional about how long you scroll through social media. Set a timer if you need to. If it's the first thing you do in the morning before you get out of bed, leave your phone in another room (yes, yes, I know…it's an alarm clock…well, I suggest just buying an actual alarm clock. They do still have those around).

Start a morning ritual of a gratitude journal, prayer and meditation or exercise…doing the things that will intentionally set the right tone for your day. Doing the things that allow you to connect with your inner wisdom and the voice of Truth, before the noise from the outside world. These are the intentional rituals that allow you to learn to trust your intuition because you will actually *know* what that still small voice is saying to you.

It's kind of like how I can pick out my son's voice, in a room full of kids. When he says "mommy!" even though there are a bunch of other kids talking and saying "mommy" to their mom, I can instantly pick out his voice because I am so familiar with it. We spend time together, we talk, and my ears are attuned to him and his voice.

This is your invitation to start to spend time with the voice of Truth so that your heart can be so attuned to it, that no matter the amount of noise that is happening around you, you know it and trust it.

We cannot lead others if we cannot lead ourselves so once we begin to lead ourselves in the right direction, filling our mind and body with the right things, and listening to the voice of Truth, *that's* when the log will catch fire.

Then, and only then, can we begin to assist others, when they are ready to be unplugged and set on fire. That's when we can turn our "less" into "more" and step into the next evolution of our purpose.

Oh, and to *trust*. Trust the voice of Truth inside, that draws you to let go of the things that may be hurting you. It takes practice to slow down, stop the social scroll and truly listen to our intuition. It takes intention to let go of the habits that move you away from the reason you were put here on this planet compared to the habits in your life that move you towards that purpose and remove the hold on the things you cannot control.

Then fall. Go for it. Shine. Leap. Jump. Fly. Fall faithfully into the arms of grace that have always been there and will always be there to catch you. It's the safest place to be.

I invite you to visit **CharityMajors.com/MeantForMore.** Under this chapter, you will find a song that I hope you take a moment to listen to, a podcast about how to learn to trust your "inner wisdom" or voice of truth, along with a morning routine to help set your day up the right way.

# Chapter 7

# Sticks and Stones

> "God does not make mistakes, and He sure didn't make one when he made you."
>
> -Charity Majors
>
> #WeAreMeantForMore
> @CharityMajors

## Chapter 7

## Sticks and Stones

I remember reciting over and over, *"Sticks and stones may break my bones, but words will never hurt me."* But why did their words still hurt? Was I weak? Was I a wimp? I closed my eyes and recited the poem again to myself, "sticks and stones may break my bones, but words will never hurt me." I opened my eyes, hoping that the hurt would magically disappear. But it was still there. The pain. My heart hurt deeply. I wanted to crawl into a hole and never come out.

I had just been told I wasn't invited to play with the other little girls. #rejected #notenough #outcast #weak #alone #inadequate I also felt wrong for feeling hurt because, apparently, I wasn't supposed to feel that way since "words will never hurt me." At a young age, I stacked another brick around my little heart and attached a belief that girls didn't like me, and that I wasn't "enough" (pretty enough, smart enough, nice enough, whatever enough) to be accepted as a part of the group. I attached a belief that it was wrong to "feel" a certain way because of a popular societal belief (or a rhyme in this case). This would be considered a "splinter" if you remember back to that previous chapter.

Even as a teenager and college student, who was constantly in groups of women because I played sports and was considered a "popular girl" in high school, I was still guarded due to little experiences (more and more splinters), like the one I shared. I would show up to practice, do my job, and go back home, with the excuse I needed to finish my homework or study for a test instead of going out with the girls. When I actually did agree to go out, it was superficial and lacked depth and substance. I was guarded and never got too close. We were surface friends who could go out, have a good time, never dive deeper into our souls and truly connect, and then we would go home.

In my experience, the layering of bricks to guard my heart and holding people at an arm's length started because I felt like there was an attack on who I truly was and how God made me. What I've found is that these attacks are the assault on someone's unique design and their true self, and this attempt to keep you stuck, dim, and playing small can have many forms. It can be the hurtful words from another child, a parent, a coach, or authority figure. It can be the hurtful words you say to yourself when you look in the mirror or mess up on something. It can come through sexual and physical abuse and the taking of something that isn't theirs to take. It can be the violation and thievery of a beautiful child or woman who is taken and trapped in the sex trade and human trafficking industry.

It can come from the impossible standard of beauty that the media and magazines shoves down our throats and the feeling that you should pick a better filter or airbrush your photos better before you post them. It can be the eating disorder that someone has so that they can meet that impossible standard of beauty or maintain a little bit of control in a chaotic world.

It can be the addition that numbs what's really going on underneath. It can come from the lack of understanding of different cultures, beliefs, skin tones, and political sides. It can come from the inexhaustible temptation to compare your everyday mess with everyone's social media highlight reel.

But where is the truth in that? Where is the authenticity and the real-ness? Where is the human connection in all this surface stuff? Where is the space of healing where we can connect soul to soul and truly accept, honor, and celebrate all of our beautiful strengths and differences? The world is longing for it. Can you feel it? #itscoming

It wasn't until I became an adult that I realized the longing I had to have deeper and authentic connections with other women, including myself. I was at a point where I couldn't ignore the feeling anymore, like I had done when I was younger. But the thought of being "more than surface friends" talking about the weather with other women brought up some old feelings. I was scared.

I was scared of being rejected again—of not being invited to "play" with the girls, like I had experienced as a little girl. I was afraid of the feeling that, for whatever reason they decided, I didn't fit in. I realized the little girl inside of me still had her feelings hurt and it was holding me back from moving forward. I began to give into my heart, meet the little girl inside of me, give her the love and acceptance she so desperately wanted and it helped unpack that limiting belief. I had to do the work to remove the bricks I had stacked and start to heal the little girl's heart within me that felt that way.

I went back to those memories, back to my six year old self, the one who had been rejected and hurt. I invited God to speak to her little heart, the exact things she would have loved to hear in that moment. The acceptance. The joy. The laughter and the sense of belonging. Through this process, I was able to detach from the limiting beliefs, drew out the good lessons I learned from them, and began to disassociate from the pain through visualization and EFT techniques. It provided learning lessons and the healing process I so desperately desired. I was able to give myself, the little girl version of myself, exactly what she had desired all along.

As I began to heal, I stepped out, still scared, and joined some women's groups. Not just any groups…groups that resonated with me, the mission I believed in, and the type of women I wanted to intentionally surround myself with. It took some trial and error, but I started to find my tribe. I started to cultivate a community. I started to see how amazing women truly are. They were encouraging, supportive, bright, and beautiful. The friendships I began to develop had depth and substance. They were life-giving and soul-nourishing.

It was how I had hoped it would be. But it wasn't until I changed my personal belief and narrative around other women that I was able to step out, be vulnerable enough and okay-enough with who I was and how God made me, to surround myself with women who equally wanted to shine bright and see me shine bright. None of our bright lights intimidated the other, and in fact, we encouraged each other to shine even brighter. We were lifting each other up, drawing out the best in each other, and it felt like it's how God intended women to be together. We all held space for each other to "be…" With no expectation, without judgment, and just the allowance for the strength that comes with being vulnerable and authentic. It was, and still is, the dream of sisterhood and tribe I always believed it could be. Dance parties, business retreats, masterminds, praying with and for each other, deep conversations, karaoke nights, and all.

If you desire soul sister connections like this, I encourage you to read Lori Harder's book called, "A Tribe Called Bliss." She gives a beautiful structure to creating a tribe along with guidelines for "soul assignments" and having the tribe allow for the space you need to remember who you are and why you are here. I've followed the format she outlines in her book with multiple tribes and it has been beautiful every time.

Looking back at my childhood, I still don't understand why we tell kids to recite the little rhymes that are the exact opposite of truth. Yes, sticks and stones may break my bones. I have two younger brothers, so I know how bad sticks and stones can feel. AND words can actually hurt a lot...sometimes more than sticks and stones. And why are we meant to feel wrong for having words hurt us? Do we realize that this is causing a childhood subconscious belief that feeling hurt by words is wrong? #mykidswontbelearningthisrhyme

I finally realize that I am not wrong for having my feelings hurt by the words that someone says, and neither are you. You were not wrong for taking another brick and stacking it in front of your heart to guard it because of the hurtful words that came out of someone else's mouth when you were younger.

Where these words get dangerous is when you begin to internalize them and believe them about yourself. That you are unlovable, that you aren't worthy, that you are ugly, that you need to be perfect, that you can't show weakness, that my "butt this", and my "fat that". Because these limiting beliefs lead to a whole lot more...

From those words and beliefs sprout actions that stem from a broken identity. Actions, or a response, can show up in many ways. It can show up as anger, shame, blame, comparison, control, guarding your heart, putting on a fake mask, and never showing flaws so we appear to be perfect. These things move us away from our most authentic and beautiful self. These actions move us away from our true identity and away from love.

The beliefs that the ten out of every one hundred women who suffer from anorexia, bulimia, and binge eating that have been internalized can be traced back to childhood wounds and words from others. It starts so small and once the snowball gets rolling, it turns into something much bigger. The psychological factors that can contribute to eating disorders include low self-esteem, depression, and lack of control in one's life, feelings of inadequacy, anger, anxiety, and loneliness. These feelings create patterns within the brain and are caused by distress in one's appearance, body weight, and shape.

Eating disorders are usually developed during adolescence and can carry on through teenage years and adulthood if not properly addressed. Being a health coach and having been in the fitness industry and pageant industry, I have known girls, seen girls, and coached girls who struggle with eating disorders. It can be traced back to hurtful experiences from their past. This is why I'm *so passionate* about empowering others to release their limiting beliefs and develop their God-given identity, because I know those little seeds can lead to bearing some pretty rotten fruit.

I haven't personally battled with an eating disorder, but I can identify with the limiting beliefs that lead me to the need to control my body, my workouts, and nutrition to look and feel a certain way, especially when the world around me feels out of control. I have seen the effects of the need to control one's body when things feel out of control. I have heard the thoughts that these girls and women think about themselves and how they use food to create a feeling within them. I've even thought them myself. I guess it just wasn't my fruit to bear in this instance. #itsheartbreaking.

When did we forget how divine, how beautiful, and how powerful we truly are?

It is a slippery slope—one that a lot of girls and women struggle with. If you, or someone you know, struggle with an eating disorder or addiction, I want to encourage you to seek professional help and begin to trace back to where it started. It may stem from a belief that was attached to an action someone else did toward or against you. I also want to encourage you to begin to seek what God says about you and the assistance it will take to unpack those beliefs and reframe those thoughts of inadequacy, unworthiness, feeling ugly, isolated, shame, and never enough. Beautiful One, *you have what it takes*, and you were made in the image of a beautiful Creator. You are Divine. There is hope and light for you and your life. You have a purpose, a big one at that.

You *are #MeantForMore.*

Those who walk through the deepest darkness usually do. Remember that it takes a special kind of person to step into their life's purpose. If you are willing to say yes to the journey... It is all meant to be a part of your process, growth, and the mess that makes your message your own. Remember that part of your purpose is to find the gifts and the lessons that have come from your hardest times so that you can pass on those lessons and healing to others. The trick is learning to unpack the bricks and layers, reframe the beliefs you have to be empowering, to learn and truly own your God given strengths, abilities, and purpose, and be okay when someone throws a dart of a hurtful word at your heart because you trust that it's all happening *for you*. Your power comes when you turn it into compassion and a deeper love for where that person is at in their journey. Your power comes from when you know that, even when it gets hard, you can find the lessons because you *will* be passing the lessons on to others.

It will take work, it will be hard, and it will be #worthit. It will be worth it because the *story of your life is worth telling.* It is worth telling those who will follow suit and experience similar things in their life that they have experienced. You will be the one to offer the hope and the belief that there is a light on the other side of the darkness they are walking through. The lessons you learn and the strength that you gain from the hard times are not meant for you to keep. They are meant for you to pass on and to empower others to #shinebrighter, too.

I believe that as women, we are being called higher. Being called to more. Being called to own our fierce beauty, power, grace, and love in a way that the world has never seen. I want to invite you to take a moment to slow down, open your heart, and listen to "You Have Called Me Higher" by Sons and Daughters (visit **CharityMajors.com/ MeantForMore** and find the song under this chapter).

You are good enough to be someone else's beacon of light and hope. You are brave enough to step into the mess of your message and begin to shine a light on the dark places of your heart so that you can shine even brighter. You are beautiful – all of your strengths, all of your body, all of your heart and all of your soul. You are fearfully and wonderfully made, and every hair on your head is accounted for by a God that is not far off out in the universe, but a God who is close to your side. You are worth loving fiercely by yourself and by others. Your journey, your heart, and your life are worth it. God does not make mistakes, and He definitely didn't make one when He made you.

But the choice is yours - to own it and take on the challenge or to stay where you are. My hope and prayer is that you choose to head straight on into the fear, into the darkness, into the mess, and do the work because I truly believe you are *meant for more*. I am here, we are here as a tribe, to lift you up, support you, challenge you, encourage you, and shine bright with you. You don't have to go alone. No sticks. No stones. Only words of life and light and a sisterhood to draw out the best in you. Come, join the tribe…you will fit right in and feel at home.

Find the link to join my FREE Facebook Group at **CharityMajors.com/MeantForMoreTribe**.

*You belong.*

# Chapter 8

# Gift Bags for Everyone

> It is our light not our darkness that most frightens us. Our deepest fear is not that we are inadequate. Our deepest fear is that we are powerful beyond measure. It is our light not our darkness that most frightens us. We ask ourselves, who am I to be brilliant, gorgeous, talented and fabulous? Actually, who are you not to be? You are a child of God. Your playing small does not serve the world. There's nothing enlightened about shrinking so that other people won't feel insecure around you. We were born to make manifest the glory of God that is within us. It's not just in some of us; it's in everyone. And as we let our own light shine, we unconsciously give other people permission to do the same. As we are liberated from our own fear, Our presence automatically liberates others.
>
> -Marianna Williamson

#WeAreMeantForMore
@CharityMajors

# Chapter 8

# Gift Bags for Everyone

I hadn't eaten spicy food so what I was feeling wasn't indigestion. It was a feeling deep down in my gut, and I couldn't shake it. I was so discontent at where I was that something needed to change. Something drastic needed to happen. But why now? Why all of a sudden? I loved what I was doing as a personal trainer, nutrition, and health coach. I loved making a difference in people's lives and helping them. I loved seeing their "ah-ha" moments when they would notice changes happening in their body and in their lifestyles. I loved seeing them grow in confidence, and how that affected other areas of their lives. I loved seeing how what I taught them got passed onto the rest of their family and the ripple effect would happen. If I loved it, why was I so discontent?

Author Rebecca Campbell calls this "that annoying feeling. That inconvenient annoying niggling feeling. Try as you might, it's there. And it ain't going anywhere…and until you face it, life just throws more bait at you to awake the niggle. Face the niggle now. It might be hard at first, but it's always better in the end…"

The Bible calls it "grace lifting." It's how to know that God's divine empowerment for an assignment or season is coming to an end and He is on the move towards something new.

That's what it was. *Discontentment.*

I gave it my own name: I call it "*divine discontentment.*" Because it was more than just not being content. There was a deepness – a divine timing to it.

It's the moment you realize that you are evolving beyond what you are currently doing, and you are being drawn to the "what's next" in your life. It's the time when what used to excite you no longer brings you into a state of joy. It's when you start to dread waking up in the morning to go and do what you've been doing. It's the feeling that there is *more* in store and where you're at doesn't *fit* anymore...

But where was this feeling coming from? I was making a difference in people's lives. Why wasn't I satisfied with it? Why did I want more? Was I being selfish in wanting to make a bigger difference? Was I conceited to feel immense joy when I envisioned helping thousands and thousands of people? Was I wrong in wanting my life to count for more? In wanting it to matter when I am gone? In my desire to leave a legacy that will continue to change people's lives long after I leave this world? Was I making it about me? Who was I to want to impact the world and make a BIG difference?

I like to attribute this feeling to the core and soul need that we all have to be *significant*; the knowing in your core that what you are doing matters and that what you are living for will outlive you. I like to attribute the reason it took me so long to do anything about it was because of the internal chatter of the ego that kept me stuck where I was.

*Who was I to want to impact the world?*

*What did I have to say that anybody would listen to?*

*Who did I think I was?*

*An author who has something to say that people will listen to?*

*An expert?*

*A selfish person who wanted to be on stage?*

*Why should people listen to me?*

*Who did I think I was, anyway?*

It was conversations just like that that kept me from moving forward. Truth be told, I wasn't an author, but I had to ask myself different questions…Instead of listening to the voices and the questions that would keep me right where I was, I began to ask myself things like "why couldn't I be an author? Why couldn't I turn my blog into a business that shares the message I have been given *and* make income from it? Why couldn't I be someone who impacted and helped hundreds – and one day – thousands and thousands of people? Why not me? Why not now? Why not start

with what I have instead of thinking of all the things that I don't have *yet*...
"

Did I have hundreds of thousands of fans and followers? No, but I had a few. Did I have hundreds of thousands of dollars in the bank? No, but I had some. Did I know everything it would take to start a blog and figure out affiliate links or even how to write what's in my head onto a website? No, but I had Google. Did I know how the heck to set up sales funnels that could house my digital products and online classrooms? No, so I got a mentor.

What about you? What are you not starting or building because you either don't know where to start or you think that you have to have this huge elaborate business plan or marketing strategy to make you an automatic New York Time's Best Seller? Here's the thing...when you start with what you have, you begin to build what you need for the future dreams. You may have dreams to be on Oprah, to be published by a major publisher, to be invited to speak to a room of 10,000 people...but can your business really – and I mean *really* – handle that right now? Maybe, maybe not. I know for me, although I would absolutely *love* for those things that I just mentioned to happen, if I am truly being honest, I don't know if I could actually handle something like that...but I know that I *will be* as I continue to grow, learn, and implement systems and a team that can help me handle those big scary and amazing dreams that I have. This is the "gap" of not being where I used to be, but not quite where I want to be...

God's timing is *always* perfect so start with what you have, do your part, and allow Him to do His part. Those dreams in your heart, that you have been holding onto ever since you were little, are not there by accident.

Growing up, I remember what it was like to have a home phone and to have all my friend's numbers memorized. I remember what it was like to leave a message on an answering machine or walk to my friend's house to see if they wanted to play. I remember what it was like to finally get our first home computer and have dial-up internet. I still remember the sound it made when it started up and the fact that we couldn't use our home phone while someone was on the internet. I remember the first time we got a cell phone and when it finally got caller-ID so we could see who was calling. I remember when Facebook started and some of us even resisted because who had time to be on that face-space-thing to see when people were going to the gym or eating avocado toast...who cared? #idoloveavocadotoast

Nowadays, it seems like anything goes. People post about their vacations, their kids, their work, and how they can't wait for the weekend. They post pictures of their cats, pictures of their feet in the sand while on vacation to make the rest of their friends jealous that they aren't on vacation, too. There are videos that go viral, articles that get shared, inspirational quotes, and passive aggressive rants that go on. There is a lot of information and a lot of noise. How do you sort through the noise online? More importantly, how do you sort through the noise in your head? Your head is filled with more information than you know what to do with. It's almost like there are millions of old school computers all logging into the internet at once. Reeeeeeeeewwwwwwaaaaaaaaaaaaaaaa...

You have news at your fingertips, tweets that share the latest reality TV show drama, Instagram to show your fancy latte with a heart on the top of it, and Live Video to have random Q & A's with anybody around the world and everyone has some advice to give. There are more personal development books, podcasts, blogs, and vlogs than you have time to read, listen to, and watch.

Yet why are so many of us still stuck either in the *divine discontentment* of what has become our lives, or stuck in a place where we have buried that desire to do more, be more, and leave a legacy because we have made ourselves believe that this is just the way life is? When did we lie to ourselves and begin to believe that having a job that we don't like, feeling "just ok" most of the time, numbing ourselves every day with Netflix marathons, a few glasses of wine, and mindless social media scrolling, being buried in debt and student loans, and never being able to keep up with the Jones' (but, by God, I'm going to try) is the status quo? We don't jump into "the gap" of transition because, frankly, it scares the crap out of our ego.

In true rebel fashion, I began to question the status quo. I cannon balled into the gap. I began to follow the flow of grace and divine discontentment – the cry of my soul that I couldn't ignore and to dig until I started to unearth the message that was buried inside. I began to follow God's leading, follow my heart and uncover my God-given strengths, gifts, abilities, likes, and dislikes. As you are experiencing by even simply reading this book, I made steps toward living fully alive in my true purpose. It was always a dream of mine to be an author, so from the bottom of my heart, thank you for reading this and for being a part of the dream. #youaremyfavorite

I'll admit, even today as you read this, I haven't "arrived", nor will I ever. The gap is still real. Have I started to unapologetically pursue the big dreams that I believe I am here for? Absolutely! Is it always smooth sailing and best sellers and millions of dollars and thousands of lives? Not hardly. It is a process. It is something that I will continue to build and rebuild so that when the time is right, when the flood gates open, when the snowflakes turn into more than snowballs and actually turn into an avalanche, I will be prepared. And it's because I am doing my part, right now, in baby steps, with what I have. And trusting God along the way.

I believe that a person's purpose is something that evolves and grows as they do, and to continue to grow, they must be willing to do the work, even when it's small, and to unapologetically (and usually afraid), jump into the gape, step into that purpose, despite what others may say or think or post or do. They have to authentically own it, as scary as it may be. Own our story, our mess, our faults, and our failures. Own your *human-ness* in all its capacity and be okay with it. Feel the fear, the anger, the jealousy, the self-doubt, the shame, the judgment, and the not enough. Feel it, accept it as a part of being human, give that part of your soul some healing, give yourself a big dose of grace, and step into that next level of power and love. And do what you can do with what you have.

I believe life is not only about owning the worst parts of us, but also owning the best parts. So many times, we can focus on the worst, the negative, the faults, and shortcomings that we forget that we *actually are* pretty amazing. I believe it's about owning that we, that I, that YOU *are* beautiful in every way. Owning that you *are* smart, powerful, kind, worthy, chosen, called, gifted, you are enough, and you have what it takes.

But how do we figure that out? How do we figure out "what we have" to actually start with? How do you know what you've been "gifted" with as a human being? How do you know what is a talent or a weakness or something that you're just not even supposed to worry about? How do you sort through the things you aren't naturally good at compared to the things that you are? What I've found is that we tend to group "gifts and talents" together in the same obscure category. I don't know about you, but for me, this was always a little muddy. What the heck did it mean, that I was "gifted and talented?"

I was at a women's conference when one of the speakers explained it in a way I had never heard (or maybe I was finally ready to hear that message at that exact time). The way she explained "gifts and talents" made total sense to me, so I'll share it with you, in hopes that if the waters are muddy for you in this area, this can give a little fresh insight.

Gifts are the things you have been good at your entire life. Imagine being a little kid... What were you naturally drawn to do, say, share, speak, read, etc.? Imagine being back in your childhood because that's back before you learned what society's standards were of you and began to act and do things according to those standards. If you look at a child, they are the true expression of what it means to be alive and in wonder of the world around you.

When I watch my son, Judah, the way he absorbs everything around him, reads books, learns words, studies people and faces, and watches everything, he is looking at the world as the new experience that it is to him. Even as a toddler Judah is very mechanical and detail oriented, and I have no doubt he will be doing something brilliant with his hands and the focus he has. He loves hard like his mama, and he lights up a room like his daddy.

If you imagine being back in that childhood stage of your life, what did you love? What were you naturally good at? The things you didn't even have to try or practice or pretend to love? What did your soul feel "at home" in while you were doing it? What brings you *joy* – true, authentic, giddy joy? What do you do that you get "lost" in...the thing(s) that you do that it feels like a few minutes have passed but you've been doing it for hours? You feel focused, alive, joyful, and *in flow*.

For me, I remember when I was a little girl, reading and writing all the time. I read books like crazy, wrote poetry and wrote in my journal all the time. I also loved to be in front of a camera. Friends would come over for play dates, and we would play "news channel." We would use my parent's HUGE (and when I say huge, I mean the size of a big diaper bag) home video camera, and we would pretend like we were newscasters. We would talk about the weather, we would joke together, and make a full show and production.

Maybe I should dig an old VHS up, get it converted to a digital video and upload it to my YouTube Channel (or maybe not)! Another thing that I loved and that came naturally to me when I was little was the ability to sing, be on stage, and share something with the audience in a microphone. I was a part of a traveling dance, singing, and performance team all throughout my childhood. I was comfortable. I felt at home and alive when I did. #inflow

People would come up to me and ask how come, even at such a young age, I wasn't scared to share my story in the microphone or sing a solo in front of thousands of people. I just wasn't... It was a gift I was given. When I'm on stage, even to this day, the peace and "alive-ness" I feel makes me feel like my soul is at home.

I wasn't always comfortable with the feeling of being comfortable on stage though. I went through a period of time where I felt wrong for feeling alive on stage or when I wrote or sang. I felt selfish, self-absorbed, and like I should really just be a good quiet girl that didn't feel alive in the spotlight or leading from the front of the room.

This is where things can get tricky. There will be an attempt, by the darkness, to have you not discover or claim your gifts. There will be lies you will tell yourself, people that will say negative things, and resistance that you will face. The amazing thing about this "tricky" part is that it's actually all happening *for* you, to build your strength, to assist you in crafting your message, to grow your story, and to put the pieces in place that you will use all along the way.

I was a first-born child. Although I started out a little rough in the beginning, I was a natural leader. (I was a very bossy big sister... Sorry, brothers!) I naturally took charge in situations at school, I was often the team captain, and even in my college party days, I was given the nickname "mother hen" because I would always make sure my friends were close by and safe.

I also loved creating and holding a space of depth and substance between friends (the actual friends who I allowed in) – a safe place where walls could come down, connections could be made, and souls could shine. I would bring people together and start to ask the deeper questions that drew out someone's hopes, dreams, and potential. I found that within that kind of space, we are truly human – in all our beautiful flaws, with no judgment, and we have permission to just be who we truly are. The assault on this gift of mine was receiving hurtful wounds, especially from women. It's usually in the points of our pain that our greatest gifts lie.

Another gift I was given is my beauty. God blessed me with an appearance that is aesthetically pleasing to today's standards of society. I used to think this was a mistake, and I didn't like looking or feeling pretty, much less actually admit it because well, "us women just shouldn't do that." I am finally at home with my authentic beauty, and I know that there is a reason for it (other than winning beauty pageants). I know that I am good in front of a still and video camera, and I can use these tools and this gift to share hope and life and light in a world that needs so desperately to know they are truly beautiful.

I will give this warning: when you begin to discover and own your God given gifts, like I mentioned, there are forces that will come against you and try to discourage you from using them. I am saying this because I have experienced this very thing, and I have heard countless stories of other people experiencing this as well. Maybe you can look back, and as you start to recognize your gifts, you can also start to recognize where they have tried to be stifled and held back. Whether these forces are the hurtful words from others or the self-sabotaging thoughts you tell yourself, or even the truly dark spiritual forces that hold you back, they are real, and they will try and keep you from fiercely owning your gifts, stepping into your purpose, and living from a place of power, abundance, light, and love.

When you start to fully and powerfully step into the gifts that God has given you, you become dangerous to the darkness. You and your light become so blinding to the darkness that it has no choice but to flee. You become a threat, and a very effective one at it, I might add.

I used to really battle with feeling wrong for liking being in front of people or being a leader, for liking to sing or speak life into someone's heart. I used to feel like I was wrong and selfish and narcissistic for wanting to do those things on a stage or from a place of influence. I still hear those self-sabotaging thoughts that try to hold me back from writing or speaking or singing or creating courses or safe spaces for women to let down their guards, connect and own their God-given gifts. I still get stuck. I still struggle. And that's okay. It's a process...it will be for you, too. It is our jobs, as those who believe we are *meant for more*, to continue on in the journey so that those who are sure to follow, will have someone worth following. To be worth following, we must first understand that *we* are the gift. Our life, our lessons, our point of view, the love we have, the message we hold...*we* are the gift.

*You* are the gift.

Now that we understand gifts a bit more, let's move on to talents. Talents are things that we have to work at. Now, it's not to say that we shouldn't and don't have to continue to refine and develop our natural gifts. It just means that refining our gifts will come easier than refining our talents. An example of a talent is cooking. Cooking, for some, may be a gift. When I was recently getting my nails done, I saw a kid's cooking show on TV. I was so impressed by these five-year-olds who whipped up these extravagant dishes with ingredients I've never even heard of, and they loved it. Cooking, for those kids, is a gift.

For me, cooking is *not* a gift. #dontjudge Now don't get me wrong, I can follow directions and a recipe will turn out great, but I'm not naturally gifted at cooking. I can't just whip up a gourmet meal with a dash of this and a pinch of that. I haven't done it enough for this talent to grow to the point where it feels natural and creative. Maybe one day I will develop my talent of cooking into something that comes more naturally, but for now, my husband is the chef, I take poopy-diaper duty, and we all eventually enjoy a great meal together.

Talents are the things and skills that you learn along the way. We tend to fumble through these, they are messy at first, and we have to get through the awkwardness of a learning curve. There is absolutely a place in your life for talents, so please don't just drop everything that you have to learn in life and only focus on your gifts. Learning and developing talents will be something that serves you for the rest of your life. An example of this is marketing and social media. I didn't always know how to market or use social media or blog or use YouTube. I had to learn. I had to get in the trenches, get my hands dirty, Google, take courses, get coaches, and fumble forward in the process. I had to do (and still do) a lot of things wrong before I started to get some of it right. I'm still no expert and there are always new technologies and strategies that come out, so staying on top of those things is the continued evolution of this talent.

Another great way to begin to understand your strengths, or "superpowers," as my friend Sheli Gartman, CEO and Founder of Women Ignite, likes to say is by taking the Gallup Strengths Finder Test. This is a ground-breaking test where you answer questions and it puts 34 different strengths in order. The amazing part about this test is that it "describes specific patterns of thought, feelings, or behavior that can be productively applied. These talents are specific enough to warrant their own definitions, their own expectations, and their own successful outcomes...Your strengths are listed in order of intensity, making the combination of your talents even more distinctive. If you wanted to find someone with the same top five themes in the same order as you, the odds are one in 33.4 million." (4)

This means that the strengths that you have, and the way that you can apply them to the world around you is unique to you. You are special. You were made to stand out from the crowd, and to use your superpowers in only the way that you can. The enlightenment that comes from taking this test allows you to focus on your strengths instead of working on your weaknesses. When you focus on your strengths verses your weaknesses, you will see exponential growth much faster!

I remember the first time I took the Strengths Finder Test. After seeing what my top strengths were, it gave me permission to be "at home" in my strengths and not feel wrong for doing something a certain way or thinking a certain way. One of my top ten strengths is Positivity. Like I mentioned before, some people tried to tear me down for being "too positive." But guess what? Now that I know it's a strength of mine, it doesn't matter that they think I live in "Positivity La-La Land" and ride magical unicorns. I own and love the fact that it's a strength of mine to be able to see the best in a situation and to see and draw out the best in others.

Another strength I have is called Maximizer. It means that I can take something that has good potential and make it great. I am confident in my ability to bring someone from good to great by seeing the potential inside of them. My Connectedness strength allows me to be great at spiritually connecting people together and holding a space where they can be safe. Pair these with my other Strategic strength and I can give strategic steps on how to get to a desired outcome.

Knowing these things about me is part of what makes me confident in my ability to lead, write, mentor and disciple, facilitate workshops, develop community, and create trainings for other people to learn from. I was made for this, and my entire being feels alive and in alignment with my true self when I am functioning within these spaces where my strengths can shine through. Knowing about how uniquely designed we all are also gives me insight to see the gifts in other people. And as I focused on these strengths of mine, (instead of my weaknesses), growth and momentum happened at an incredible rate.

It's an amazing feeling to be able to speak to the potential within someone and to genuinely see – and call out – the greatness that's inside. Once you begin to see your unique design, you will be able to see it in others and truly be grateful for every single person you come in contact with (yes, even the ones that may try and tear you down). And *that* is when the magic happens…

I want to invite you to take the Gallup Strengths Finders test by visiting **CharityMajors.com/ MeantForMore** and follow the link from this chapter.

I encourage you to take some time away from the noise, the social media, and the hustle and bustle and begin to sift through the things that are gifts and talents in your life. Quit trying to improve your weaknesses. Focus on your strengths. What were you naturally good at as a child? What did you love? What lit you up and gave you the authentic joy that you see on a child's face? Ask your family. Ask your childhood friends. Ask the child inside of you. I also believe that tears reveal destiny so what moves your heart to tears?

As you begin to pinpoint those things, if you aren't already, begin to incorporate those things into your life. Remember, start where you are with what you have. It may look like taking piano lessons again or getting a new cookbook. It may mean volunteering with children or starting to host a group of friends once a month at your house (or a book club with this book), so you can connect and teach and create a safe space. It may mean you begin to write again, start a blog or a YouTube Channel, or set aside money, so you can take that adventure you always wanted to.

Beginning to own your gifts means that you need to make space in your day and be intentional about incorporating those things in your life. It won't happen by accident and you may experience some resistance as you begin to bring back the joy and light into your life. It's okay. And guess what? #youareworthit Your light, your gifts, you fully alive and in alignment with why you are here on this planet, is needed in this world. We need you - all of you - in all of your brightness, unapologetically shining for others to see.

Everyone is waiting for someone else to go first, so be brave. #gofirst

Do the thing, create the thing, write the thing, or build the thing.

Whatever it is.

Whatever gifts you have been given, use them.

The world is waiting...

*And also remember...YOU* are a gift...so give yourself – your story, your lessons, message, yourself – to the world.

Jesus said that He came to the world to serve, not to be served...So in a world that says "this is (or isn't) serving me, **serve.**

## Chapter 9

# Bring on the Arrows

> "To avoid criticism, say nothing, do nothing, be nothing."
>
> —Unknown

#WeAreMeantForMore
@CharityMajors

# Chapter 9

# Bring on the Arrows

Arrows, darts, and death by a thousand cuts - all sound torturous and not very fun. Unfortunately, as we have learned in this book and through experiences in life, wounds, big and small, happen. We are human, we are messy, we won't always get it right, and neither will those around us. It's important to understand this common knowledge…and not just know it but also truly understand it at a core level.

Studies show that the human brain likes things to connect and make sense of things. When something doesn't make sense, brain activity amps up and fills in the blanks along the way. The "blanks" are based on that individual's past experiences and subconscious understanding of the world around them.

Here is an example. Imagine being in a house, and a dog comes running through the door. He is soaking wet, dripping all over the floor. The dog comes running around the corner in the house, brushes against your leg, shakes the water off, heads towards his water bowl and begins to drink.

Now I'll ask you: what kind of dog was it? What color was the floor of the house? What kind of pants were you wearing when the dog rubbed up against your leg? What type of water bowl was it?

As your brain filled in the parts of this story, it is based on your past experiences. Maybe you saw a golden retriever dog or a lab or a yorkie or your childhood dog. Maybe the floor of the house was carpet to one person but to someone else, it is hardwood. Some people picture themselves wearing jeans, some picture slacks, and if you're my son, I'm pretty sure he would picture himself in just a diaper because he loves to be "nakie-baby." Was the water bowl metal or wood or plastic or some other type of bowl that you have seen somewhere?

See how we can take the same story, but because of all of our different life experiences as individual humans, our brain fills in the blanks differently? This is a big reason why people misunderstand each other, especially when it comes to different beliefs, skin colors, political sides, backgrounds, and what we post on social media.

I was meeting with a new client who was going through one of my Transformation Coaching Programs. She was excited and ready to step into a new level of confidence, get equipped with tools to help her grow in her identity and the gifts she had. When we met, she admitted something to me. She admitted that she was scared to meet with me, but it wasn't because of who I was. It was because of who I represented to her. #itsnotyouitsme

Because of my looks, to her, I represented the "popular girls" in high school that teased her, hurt her and rejected her. She had done enough personal growth to understand that it wasn't *who I was* that brought up these feelings, but it was because of her past experiences.

My internal monologue said, "Oh great, apparently *I* represent rejection to everyone around me because of the "mean girls" in high school... grrreeeeaaattttt... that explains a lot..." (Side note - Ladies, can we change this stereotype? What if the pretty girls were also the nice girls? What if *all* girls were confident, loving, beautiful, and encouraging? What a beautiful world that would be...#mydream #mymission).

I thanked my client for her honesty, and it also got me thinking. How many times do we put someone we don't even know, into a certain box or category, just because they trigger something in us that was in a past experience? What boxes have I put others in? And what boxes was I being put in by others based on their past experiences?

This became a big #ahamoment for me and I began to understand the power of perception at an even deeper level. Oh, our beautiful brains and how they fill in the blanks...

The unfortunate part about our brains doing this is that the story it fills in is based on our past experience (remember the dog running through the house example?), which is damaged and never perfect. The story we tell ourselves is usually the worst story possible instead of giving the person the benefit of the doubt. Have you ever called or texted someone and they didn't get back to you? What was the story you started to tell yourself? Are they mad at me? What did I do? They don't like me. #blahblahblah.

In light of this knowledge, I propose this question: if our brains are going to make up a story anyways, what happens if we were to tell ourselves a different story? What if we were to believe the best about the other person (and ourselves) instead of the opposite? Why not *choose* a different story? Why not *intentionally* fill in the blanks with the best possible outcome, the happiest of details, and anything else that leads us back to love. Love for ourselves, for others, for our planet, and love for God.

Author Don Miguel Ruiz talks about this in his book, "The Four Agreements." The second agreement that Ruiz writes about is "Don't Take Anything Personally." This is all about understanding that nothing that others do is because of you and what others say and do is a projection of their own reality. I highly recommend diving into this book and implementing these four agreements into your life.

Not taking things personally is something that we can *all* work on. It's something that I remind myself of, as well as my husband. My husband gets minor bursts of road rage when he drives. The stories he comes up with about the other drivers are sometimes comical and other times very "interesting." Not too long ago, we were driving to one of our favorite vacation spots. The road that leads up to the mountains is pretty narrow and winding. There are a few passing lanes, but for the most part, drivers tend to file in behind each other and hunker down for the curvy ride ahead. On this trip, there were a few cars following close to each other. Behind my cute white SUV mom-car, that my husband was driving, was a big black pickup truck, with massive lifted tires, tinted windows, a big front grill and a really loud engine.

A few cars, including us, were playing the "wait for the passing lane and floor it" game to pass a few slower cars and this big pickup truck behind us was doing the same. We finally made it to the front of the line, with the pickup close behind. At the next passing lane, the pickup floored it, the engine blasted through the mountain canyon, and they pulled up next to us, trying to pass. In the other lane ahead of us, a car came around the corner; the pickup saw them, slowed back down and pulled in behind us again.

My husband's eyes bugged out a bit and he began to say how big of an idiot that guy was, how his big truck was "compensating for something that was smaller," and how he was going to get out of the car and have some choice words with the guy in the pickup. I laughed. I couldn't help it. I questioned why he was taking it so personally... I thought he was just trying to pass. Sure, maybe it was louder because of whatever fancy muffler was on the truck, but for some reason, my husband took offense and wanted to kick the guy's butt.

A few more curves in the road and another passing lane, the truck behind us floored it again and passed safely and loudly. The pickup driver got the stare of death from my husband, who I'm sure if he could, would have shot laser beams out of his eyeballs and blown up the big black truck. I laughed again, as this time, Chris began to make up another story about how the guy was a huge jerk, how he probably wasn't very smart and never graduated high school or driver's education for that matter and mumbled a bit more about big tires and big trucks overcompensate for tiny "things." I laughed it off, told him to relax, and I changed the subject.

Although I'm no psychologist and I'm definitely not my husband's "breakthrough buddy" (he can get his own therapist for that), and it's not my job to fix him, I wondered what it was about that truck that made my husband feel insecure or threatened and feel the need to lash out in a way that made him feel better about himself. Was it the loudness of the engine? The big tall grill in the rearview mirror? Was he picked on in high school by a guy with a similar truck? Was it the tinted windows that guarded the true identity of the other driver? Why was he taking it so personally?

How many people around us seem like the "big truck?" Are there people who are really loud and proud? Or people who just seem to grill you all the time? What about people who hide in the shadows or keep masks up and you can never truly connect with their human spirit on the other side? Do you begin to put them down? Make assumptions about them as a person? Call them names and make them less threatening in your mind by telling yourself they are compensating for something?

Unfortunately, as human beings, we ALL do this. We all throw darts and arrows and sometimes laser beams from our eyeballs at others around us when we feel threatened or inferior. It's a natural response to protect yourself and make the other person feel inferior in your own mind. Especially when someone is in the public eye…

As a public figure and a community activist, everything I do, say, wear, write, and post is under a microscope. That is the cost of being in the public eye and being an influential person in a community. The interesting thing I find about being a leader is that leaders also tend to be targets. They tend to be who people judge the quickest, who gets criticized the most, and whose actions are often misunderstood or misperceived. The bright light that attracts the bugs.

During my pursuit to Mrs. America, I had posted a short video in a business Facebook group. I was in between appointments, I was driving to my next meeting, and needed to ask businesses for some silent auction items for a non-profit event that we were doing. Having my headphones in and having a dashboard phone holder (since I like to practice safety and not hold the phone while I drive), I pushed record and and did a quick video asking for businesses to donate for the cause and posted it in the group at the next red light.

Little did I know that my "recording while driving" post would create a frenzy. One man, in particular, began to criticize me for not being a safe driver, for being a bad example to children, and that I shouldn't be looked at as a role model. This man took it upon himself to shame me as much as he could by contacting every news station, every newspaper, and posting about how bad of a person I was on many social media professional pages and Facebook groups.

These things really hurt me because in all my "good and safe intention," to collect items for children with cancer, I didn't think my video was that big of a deal. I had the phone dash-holder, I kept both hands on the wheel, I kept my eyes on the road, I used the headphones, and didn't feel any different as if I was talking to someone next to me in the car. But I had to take a step back and look at it objectively. Did my actions align with my intentions? Every leader and influencer needs to at one point or another.

Yes, as a public figure, everything I do is an example to others. As an influencer and someone that knows they are *meant for more,* your actions are too. I took down my own defenses and justifications and admitted that it wasn't the best of examples to record a video while driving, and I should have chosen a better time to do it. I swallowed my pride, took down the post and publicly apologized. But I didn't stop there (my brain seldom does).

I began to wonder why this one man was so adamant about "attacking me" all over the place. Seek to understand first, before being understood, right? After some Googling and Facebook stalking, I found out that a distracted driver had severely injured one of his family members in a car accident. I suddenly saw what it was like to be in his shoes and understood where his passion was coming from. It made a lot more sense to me, and I began to seek ways to turn a negative situation around.

From my heart felt vulnerability and *very* public apology (which was also featured on the news) came more support, prayers, love and encouragement than I could have imagined. Through my example of humility as a leader, admitting I was wrong and showing this man compassion, others were inspired. They saw how I handled a not-so-positive situation.

I was also able to turn this bad publicity around by being proactive, connecting with the Department of Transportation and a few news stations and co-promote a public and social media movement against distracted driving. Maybe lives were saved from the greater awareness that this entire situation brought to distracted driving. I like to think it did. (PS - use my example and *don't* record videos while driving...but for real...just don't). #justdrive

This situation was a good reminder that I *am* an example, I *am* a leader, and I *am* held to a higher standard. And I need to be okay with that. My word and actions need to be in integrity. As a forward facing public figure, I need to be okay with having a microscope on what I do, and I also need to be strong enough to take the arrows that will undoubtedly come my way. And I need to be aware enough of when it's time to take a negative situation and turn it around for good.

And so do you. *#WeAreMeantforMore*

These things come with the territory of being *meant for more*. If I let myself, knowing this it can be something that keeps me playing small. It can be something that I don't want to deal with. It's hard to be misunderstood. It's hard to be judged by people that only see snapshots of your life. It makes me want to stay safe and in my own little world. *Or*...I can accept the calling that is on my life to be an influencer, a leader and a public servant, and hold myself to that higher standard.

**You** will have to make that choice, too. *#WeAreMeantForMore*

It hasn't always been this way though...I wasn't always ok with the knowledge that with my life's purpose will also come difficulty...

Throughout my life, I have experienced dart after dart, laser beam after laser beam, and judgment after judgment. So much so, that there was a time in my life where I was scared to even do anything or say anything to other people because everyone around me seemed to be misinterpreting and misunderstanding me completely.

I began to play small, keep to myself, and walk on eggshells in fear of anyone misjudging who I was and accusing me of something I didn't do or say. It was like no matter what I did, their brain "filled in the spaces" of my life and who I was as a person with the worst-case scenario. And every time it happened, it boggled my mind, hurt my feelings, and caused me to dim my light even more. My light was under heavy attack.

I have been accused of implying that my husband was better than another girls' husband because I posted a picture on Facebook of flowers that my husband got me. I have been accused of trashing another girl's personal core religious beliefs and attacking her as a person with a live video that I did about eating healthy things like fruits, vegetables and lean organic meats. I have been given nicknames like Volleyball Barbie because I wore a ribbon in my ponytail, Mrs. Potato Head when I was Mrs. Idaho, selfish, a narcissist, little Miss Perfect, greedy, manipulative, stupid, conceded, and Mrs. Positivity that lives in "Positivity-La-La Land".

What hurts the most is that these things, these accusations, these judgments, couldn't be farther from the truth. They are so uncharacteristic of me, who I am, how I was raised, how I treat people, and my core beliefs that it boggles my mind how someone could even think or say things like that about another person. The recurring pattern of hurt in my life has been based on misperception and insecurities, which I now know is helping others to see themselves and others through the lens of love (heck, that's even what my name means). #loveisthekey

Despite the arrows thrown, I remember the power of perception, and how our brain fills in the blanks. I begin to feel empathy and compassion towards that person who is shooting arrows at me because in reality, they are hurting – probably due to some situation in their past - and I am the target of their hurt for whatever it was that I did or how I look that triggered them. It's not to say that I don't take feedback, because I do. I want to continue to get better and grow. I also know that not everyone's criticism or opinion deserves my attention.

I invite you to begin to see those who have thrown arrows at you in the same way. There is something about you that triggers something in them and once you can understand that what they see in you is actually what's going on within them, it changes everything.

It helped me step out of victim mode and into a mindset of compassion for that other person. It helped me to know how to pray for them, and to take time to check myself, my actions, my intentions, and how others may perceive them. I am not, nor will I ever be perfect...no one will...we will all mess up, we won't get something right, and that's ok. It is our job to do the best we can with what we have and to be mindful to come from a place of love and pure intention in the things that we do and things we create.

My favorite book (the Bible) says that "no weapon formed against me will prosper," but it doesn't say that there will be no weapons that are formed. Although they won't prosper, weapons *will* be formed.

So even in my good intentions and solid character, arrows have been thrown at my character, my integrity, and who I am as a leader, wife, mom, person... Those are the arrows that hurt me the most. I can handle if someone calls me a silly name or says my hair looks bad or they don't like my clothes (at least now I can). It's when someone makes a remark about *who I am* that really hurts. I *know* I'm not a bad person. I *know* that I genuinely love people and would do anything for others. I am loyal and kind; I am generous, fun loving, easy-going, confident, passionate and driven. I know that I'm not perfect, and that I'm trying my best.

And I believe that others are, too.

It took me a long time, a lot of work, a lot of prayer, and a ton of personal development to start to stand firm in who I was, not play small, to be paralyzed in fear and not worry about what others may say. I'll admit, it still hurts my feelings if someone says something negative about me, but I'm getting stronger and stronger every day and try and pray for that person instead of letting my mind shoot laser beams back at them.

I'll admit something else to you... I'm scared, even as I write this book, that people will throw arrows and darts at me for sharing my story, for being vulnerable, for challenging you to grow, for shining a light, even on what can seem insignificant to some. It's scary to "put it all out there" for the world to see and read and judge and fill in their own blanks.

The negative voices in my head scream loud and clear and say, "who do you think you are," "they're never going to like this," "you're not a good enough writer," "they are going to judge you even more…" It's scary, but I know I need to do it. Not for me (well, partially for me), but mostly for the one girl's life that this book might encourage. The one woman's heart that needs to hear that she is beautiful. The one person's purpose that has not yet been stepped into because they have been ridiculed like I have been. The light that has been dimmed and the heart that has the wounds from taking arrows.

It's for *you*.

It's for *me*.

It's for **us.**

It's scary, but I know I must share it anyway.

As I lean into the fear, do multiple dance parties to psyche myself up, and despite the negative voices swirling around in my head, I know I must keep tuning into my voice of truth, keep writing and keep shining a light because we, as human beings, need to walk through the healing of the things we keep hidden in the dark. The first step to this is awareness. So here I am, flashlight in hand, scared and trying to make friends with my yelling ego, and sharing these words in hope that we, one by one, and eventually as a human race, can all begin to move toward believing the best about others.

Truly loving one another in our unique design, instead of throwing arrows and darts at one another in hopes that the other person won't threaten our existence.

I believe in a world where a woman's beauty is not a threat to another woman. I believe in a world where, when someone does something new, her friends don't try to tear her down for it. I believe in a world where our flaws and failures are actually what make us perfect. I believe in a world where masks are trampled on by the power of vulnerability and authenticity. I believe in a world where men are not threatened by a woman who has fully owned her greatness. I believe in a world where women champion other women, where we collaborate instead of compete, and where we truly embrace the fierce power that is within us to make the world a beautifully better place.

In a perfect world (which I know doesn't exist on this side of eternity), that's what it would be like. It would be like nature – like a field of wildflowers – where one flower isn't intimidated by the blooming of another flower next to it. They all just bloom – in all their brilliance... together...beautifully together.

But since we are on this side of eternity, we need to understand that arrows will come, darts will be thrown, laser beams will be shot out of judgmental eyes, and we pretty much have to get stronger and be okay with it because it will all still be worked out for our good.

We (myself included), *cannot* play small, can't "say the thing" or "do the thing" or "create the thing" in fear that someone will judge us. It's going to happen regardless, so go BIG, Girl.

A mentor of mine, Lori Harder, says to "choose your future self now…" (listen to her inspiring podcast, linked at **CharityMajors.com/MeantForMore**).

Hold yourself to a higher standard and go BIG, go all out, go for it, do it afraid, and shine brighter than ever before. Arrows and all. We are strong enough. You are strong enough. You have what it takes. You were divinely created and uniquely designed to handle what comes your way and to use it for the good of others. You are here for just a time as this. You *are* meant for more…

So shine, Beautiful One…***STEP IN, STEP UP, SHINE.***

# Chapter 10

# Why, Yes, I'll Have Another...

> "At some point, there comes a time where you have to shift your focus from what has happened to what is next."
>
> -Unknown
>
> #WeAreMeantForMore
> @CharityMajors

# Chapter 10

# Why, Yes, I'll Have Another...

Despite how awesome things look on the outside, I've "been *there.*" Depressed. Down. Drowning. As I've shared in previous chapters, I've experienced the deepest low of what it means to literally not get out of bed or have the desire to go on. I've been at the point of numbing myself with a bottle of wine. It felt better than the present pain of being aware that I didn't even have the energy to think, pray, smile, feel the pain, get up out of bed, or do anything but stare at the wall.

Depression is a *real thing* that feels so isolating. The truth is, that I wasn't alone, even though it felt that way. Almost 15 million people in the United States suffer from depression.

Depression can be caused by a multitude of things, especially today where it is so easy to scroll through social media and see all the highlight reels of everyone else's lives, all the while we are in sweat pants, haven't showered, the house is a mess and it's Friday night. *Awesome. I'm such a party animal!*

For me, one of my seasons of depression set in after coming out of a position that fueled my deeper purpose. I had been in a public figure leadership position for the term of the year, and I felt more alive during that year than I had in a long time. I was thriving in my service to the community, I was in leadership positions, and I was gaining recognition for my contribution. It made me feel good. I was serving, growing, leading, learning, and loving it. Every part of me felt alive.

I understood the position was only for a year, so I wanted to make the most out of it. It was a very high energy season of life where I was very "outward facing" or, very focused on being out in public. Having done a lot during that time in terms of community service, networking, speaking, growing influence, etc., I also tried to prepare myself for the end of it (or so I thought). I either hadn't prepared enough or I didn't know the extent of how far down I would sink. I figured there would be a natural emotional/physical/mental "low" after such a high point, but why had I sunk so far? The "inward facing" season had started. It was time to do the flow that comes with the ebb and focus a bit more on my inward world. This natural correction of eb and flow energy was lower and more inward than I thought it would be...how was I ever going to get back to the "upswing" and flowin' again?

Being *meant for more* means that we need to honor the different seasons we will journey through. If you imagine the four seasons of the year, not everything is in growth and harvest all the time. There are seasons of things falling away and dormancy. As an influencer, it is important to recognize the seasons when we are to be "outward facing" and those where we are to be "inward facing."

Honoring the lows, looking for the lessons in the "inward facing seasons," – the fall and the winter – there is *always* purpose in those seasons, too, so don't discount a season of dormancy, rest, or darkness. Every season has its purpose.

During my "low," I knew it would be good for me to pray, but I didn't even have the energy to open my mouth. I knew it would be good to read, but I didn't have the mental capacity to comprehend what I was reading. I knew it would be good to listen to inspiring podcasts, but my fingers wouldn't do anything else but mindlessly scroll through social media for hours on end.

There was an interesting internal battle going on. My conscious mind knew that it was a phase - I would come out, I was stronger, I knew what would help snap me out of it and God had a big purpose still in store. But my subconscious wouldn't let me move or act on any of those promises I believed in or any of the actions that would allow me to begin to climb out.

I never felt so internally conflicted and purpose-less. I had gone through struggles before when I had graduated college. I had put so much of my identity in my position as a volleyball player that when it went away, I didn't know whom I was or what I was a part of. This time, it felt different. I was conscious of not allowing my identity to be wrapped up in the public position I held, so I couldn't figure out why this energy correction felt as drastic as it did.

Was it that I didn't know what was next? Was it that God was teaching me to honor the seasons of rest and that it's ok to be inward facing? Was it the feeling of *divine discontentment*, yet again, that was drawing me towards the next evolution of why I was here on this planet? The questions swirled, and my ego chattered more negative self-talk...again...

Why is it when we are weak that the negative self-talk that keeps us down becomes the loudest? Why is it when we need a "pick-me-up" the most that our ego and the enemy try to keep us down, play tricks on us, and tell us lies?

Had I taken the time to seek and plan out what's next or had the answer not come to me yet? Did I miss the answer? I knew I was evolving past my profession as a fitness and nutrition trainer and the couple of clients that I had were still hanging on for dear life (truth be told, they came more for the therapy and friendship than they did for the actual workout).

Was that it? That was all that I was going to amount to and that was going to be the best year of my life and it was all-downhill from there? Geez, I hoped not but the negative thoughts kept coming. *"You're all washed up now. That was the best you will ever amount to. You missed out on so many opportunities. You didn't do enough. You didn't serve enough. You didn't make the connections you needed to make. You are washed up. You shouldn't even get out of bed. What's the use of getting out of bed? You're not getting up to do anything. Here, have another glass of wine. Let's scroll and look at everyone else's happy amazing lives while you lay here in your funk...".*

My brain is quite the chatterbox…ha! But this inquisitiveness and constant asking of questions has been such a gift in the uncovering of God's divine design.

Maybe you, too, have been in the emotional winter season after an amazing summer. Maybe you, too, have heard the negative words of your ego or the enemy and you question what it all is for…

Truth be told, wine and mindlessly scrolling through social media were the only things that would shut my brain up. Normally, I'm a happy, positive, mentally strong person. What happened this time that I couldn't meditate myself out of this funk? Where did these thoughts come from? Certainly, they weren't buried below the surface in the depths of my subconscious? I've done *plenty* of work on myself and my mindset… Was it enough? Why were they there? Who put them there? And why were they all coming up at once?

It's in the pressure of life that you experience what's truly below the surface. Anyone can put on a happy face and do great things when everything is awesome. But what about when life gets hard? What about when the pressure gets tough? What about when we lose the competition, mess up the project, make the "wrong" decision, or fail?

**What's underneath will come out during pressure…**

It's kind of like the process of making wine. You don't get wine unless you squeeze the juice out of the grapes. But it's a messy process. It's a process that requires pressure, filtering, mixing, sanitizing, growth, isolation, suffocation, adjustments, and *finally* enjoying the fruits of your labor. Let me explain...

I'm no wine maker, although I do like to enjoy a glass here and there (not full bottles anymore, like I did to numb myself in that low season I mentioned before). I like to visit wineries for their delicious tapas, scenery, concerts and wine tasting. During winery tours (and Googling), I started to learn a little bit about the process of making wine. It's a bit like life, as you will find.

To make wine, certain equipment is needed. Things like jars, buckets, mesh, corks, mixing utensils, etc. There are also certain ingredients needed. Grapes, sugar, water and yeast. The process begins by choosing your grapes, washing them, and crushing them to get the juice out.

Isn't it just like life to give you certain "equipment" like your gifts and purpose, having to mix them with certain "ingredients" like your talents, your experiences and people around you mixed with the cleansing and pressure process of your life's journey?

But back to the wine... after the crushing and pressure comes the filtering. The juice of the grapes gets mixed up with the pulp, so to get the pure juice that makes the wine, the "junk" or the unwanted parts of the grape must be ran through a filtering cloth so that all that remains is the juice. Once the juice is mixed with sugar, water, and yeast, it is set aside to ferment for a period of time, and then when it's ready, it becomes the deliciousness that we call wine.

This part of the wine making process is kind of like the part of your journey when you go through something hard. The pressure brings out the juiciness of who you are, but it also brings out some of the junk. It is up to you to filter through the junk and add in the right ingredients that cause you to sweetly grow (like the yeast and sugar in the wine).

It's up to you to use the times of being alone, like wine on a shelf, to brew your best ideas, to sift through the habits, thoughts, things, and people in your life that are no longer for your best and highest good, because there may not be room for them where you are going. Once you are ready to serve others, you can do so to the best of your abilities. Just like when a great glass of wine is served, life is meant to be enjoyed, and enliven the senses through the experience of taste and aroma. It helps you let down your guard, enjoy the moment, and make good conversations and connect with others.

So, what did I do to change the direction of my energy when I was in the low and in my wine funk? Well, first, I put down the wine. That's always a great place to start. I also began to pray, journal and be active again. It wasn't much at first, but it was baby steps. Remember, there is a beautiful dance that we learn in life, to honor the dormant seasons, but also not allow ourselves to stay there.

As my wine haze faded and my mindfulness practices began to shift my energy, I also knew that serving others creates a major shift. So that's exactly what I did. I volunteered my time at places that I knew would make me grateful for where I was and everything that I had. I got involved at women's shelters and homeless shelters. I worked with teens and their emotional intelligence.

Along with service, comes the conscious effort to find the good things that come out of winter. I began to use the down time to brew my best ideas. That's where some of these chapters have come from, where my speaking training took another major leap, where I was able to dive into leadership courses, business masterminds, and entrepreneur trainings. I started to fill up my cup, so that it was overflowing again.

I used the downtime to slow down, listen to my heart and the voice of Truth about me, who I was, and where God was taking me. The dreams that I saw during that time are ones that I hold onto and continue to walk towards…including this book!

And one more thing…my hubby and I made a baby! The downtime turned into the greatest gift because I was able to focus on having a healthy, calm, stress-free pregnancy, (with lots of massages) and I have no doubt that's why my son is such a happy and sweet spirited kid. He grew in an environment full of love and care, not one full of stress and worry. (Check out the book Origins, How the Nine Months Before Birth Shape the Rest of Our Lives by Annie Murphy Paul – a link is provided in the resources for this chapter at **CharityMajors.com/MeantForMore**).

What a gift that season of life turned out to be. I found the juiciness of life in what started out as a bottle of wine.

Maybe you, like me, have experienced the inward facing season, discontentment or you're not quite sure who you are meant to be or what you're supposed to do. Although it is still a hard process to be in the middle of and it's always easier to say, "invite the wine-making process" into your life so that you can serve others at the next level of your purpose. Don't run from the winter. Embrace it. Just like a seed in winter, the magic happens below the surface. Roots grow deeper in winter. Be intentional about these seasons in life and use it to fuel the "what's next" in your purpose.

*After* winter is over, if you find yourself reaching for that bottle of wine, remember this chapter's analogy, put down the bottle and start to do the work on yourself. Find the juiciness. Embrace the process. It's all happening *for* you. The lessons are there for you to learn so that you can teach those lessons to others.

I also want to encourage you to give, volunteer and serve, even if it's volunteering at your local homeless shelter. There is nothing like serving others and being in a state of giving that snaps a person out of their funk, changes their energy, makes them grateful for where they are, and gets them back on track going towards their mission.

I encourage you to embrace the pressure and the purification process. For it's within that time that the juiciness of who you are, and the purpose God has on your life will come out. Embrace the pressure. Embrace the cleansing. Embrace the process of growth. It's all a part of your journey and your purpose.

It's how you find your *more...*

# Chapter 11

# A Magic Wand Life

> "Don't ask what the world needs. Ask what makes you come alive and go do it. Because what the world needs is people who have come alive."
>
> -Howard Thurman
>
> #WeAreMeantForMore
> @CharityMajors

# Chapter 11

# A Magic Wand Life

As we near the end of this book, I hope you have found some value as I shared the lessons I've learned through these stories, as I've shared some of what I believe can make the world a better place, and how I believe in the potential and God given purpose that is inside of *you*.

I have one last exercise I'd like for you to do with me.

Imagine I have a magic wand... (Remember, I ride unicorns in positivity la-la land, so it's not that far off to think that I can have a magic wand, too...)

I have a magic wand, and as you are reading this, I am waving it. All sorts of glitter and sparkles and unicorn sprinkles are sweetly dusting you and your life. You now have *all* of the money and *all* of the time in the world. #jackpot

The question I have for you is this: What would you *really* be doing with your life?

For real though...if you won the mega-lottery today, what would you *really* be doing with your life?

I want you to take a moment and really think about this. Maybe even journal about it. There are no right or wrong answers, and nothing is out of reach.

***If you want to:***
- *Travel to the moon...*
- *Build the largest art museum ...*
- *Take a trip around the world with your family...*
- *Give millions of dollars to save children trapped in the sex slave industry...*
- *Invent the next piece of technology that will forever change the world ...*
- *Hire a chef and a massage therapist and a hair-dresser every day of the week (that's one of mine)...*

Nothing *is out of reach.*

What would you *really* be doing with your life? How would you spend your time and your unlimited resources? Who would be there with you? How would you feel?

Dream and journal for a bit... see it in your mind's eye. Feel what it would feel like to live out your dream life. Find some images on Pinterest and make a dream-board. Post some of them to your social media and tag me so I can see them! (@CharityMajors on all platforms).

Then keep reading...

As I have asked this question over the years, I've found that most people don't allow themselves to dream this big. Most people say they would pay off their credit card and house, give to their favorite charitable organization, go on vacation for a couple weeks, and that's about it. And those are all great things...but it should be just the start. Most people that I ask literally stop their brain and imagination from getting any bigger. Why is this? When did we lose the imagination we had when we were young when we could be anything we ever wanted? When the world wasn't such a serious place and we could run around with no pants on and nobody cared. When we walked up to random people and started conversations about our poop, how good the food was at snack time, how our daddy caught us from the monkey bars, how our Barbies were all friends, and about how we just built a rocket ship out of pillows that was going to take us to the moon because that's what was going on in our lives.

I began to ask this question because someone had once asked me. When they asked me for the first time, I found that I hadn't allowed myself to dream big either. As I mentioned before, I had settled for what my current reality was and "kinda hoped that one day" the big dreams and life's purpose that I had buried deep in my heart would one day come true. I had settled for waking up, going to work, going to the grocery store and wandering the aisles, living for the weekends, posting about TGIF, hump-day Wednesdays, Throwback Thursdays, and barely making enough to pay my bills, chip away at the mountain of student loans, and Monday would roll back around.

I had settled for the grind. My "truth" (with a lower-case t, compared to a universal Truth with a capital "T") was Groundhog Day, where I would maybe get a vacation a year, a stay-cation if I was lucky, and the reality that the dreams I had when I was younger about being an author, a speaker, a world-traveler, a difference maker, and a potential igniter to thousands and thousands and even millions one day were just too farfetched and not realistic (or so I thought).

When did we stop believing that we could go, do, create, be, say, and have wherever we dreamed? When did the carefree spirit of the little girl on the playground who didn't have a care in the world?

Maybe you, like me, have felt that same way about life. Maybe you have been playing small, too, and settling for the status quo. Maybe you have said "someday", too. It's okay. There is hope, it is all happening *for* you, and when you have the inner-knowing that you are *meant for more*, it can't be ignored.

The dreams that I had buried for so long are still being uncovered and some of them still seem like a long way off (like starting an orphanage or a center that rescues women and children out of human-trafficking or working with women to build their self-confidence and unlock their purpose, to equipping the world's top leaders, to have a house in Mexico and yes, having a hair dresser do my hair. (Every. Single. Day). #itwillhappen #goals

Although I am still working toward those things that I see on my Pinterest vision board and in the big crazy dreams I see in my head, I now know that I am not limited by my current reality or what I can see that's just in front of me. I am only limited by *me*, and I'm working on getting myself out of the way so that I can be used to make an impact on the world... not for the sake of me doing something great, but for the sake of living a life that will leave something that will outlive me. For the sake of the lives and hearts that will be changed so *they* can help change the world too. Because I am simply the messenger of this message and it is my job to steward the gifts I have been given so that my life can be used in the way that God has called me to be used.

THIS is what it's all about. This is the beautiful journey of what we call life. It is *your purpose* to find your purpose and to live it out... fully, fiercely, and brightly. Who you are is your gift to you, but what you do with who you are is your gift to the world...and *yes*, **you are a gift**! What you do with the lessons that life gives you *is* your purpose. What you learn from the good times and the bad times *is* your purpose. The way you pass on those lessons to others and help them shine bright too *is* your purpose.

**The process *is* the purpose.**

I want to challenge you to do this magic wand exercise and begin to unpack the hopes and dreams that are inside of you. It may take you quite a few times to begin to allow your brain to follow the unlimited possibilities of dreaming this big. Get a journal and write it down. Nothing is too big, nothing is too farfetched. Nothing is wrong, and nothing is out of reach. Dream, Darling, for "as you dream, so shall you be."

There will be some sifting and sorting of these dreams and visions that goes on and you may begin to question, which dreams are the ones for me? Which dream has been buried in my heart, and how do I know it's what I'm supposed to pursue? Whenever you have been given a dream, it is placed deep within your heart. The Hebrew word for "heart" (or *kardiva*), literally means "the real you." Ancient writings use the word, "heart" to mean your love, your internal motivation, and your passions. When you have a God given passion for something, it literally means it is incorporated within your being. It is a part of you, and your story.

Your mess becomes your message, and it's one worth telling. You have a story that can only be told the way that you tell it. The places you fear exposure, the places you hold most sacred and protect their vulnerability, that's where your power lies. That's where the dreams are stored.

"The brightest candle gives off the biggest shadow." It's the places of your shadow that will bring out the brightest light and give you the flame to ignite others.

As you begin to dream bigger and ignite what is within you, I have one more challenge for you. I want to challenge you to write a letter to your future self.

Write yourself a letter, one that you will read one year from now, five years from now, and even ten years from now. Write it to yourself, in present and past tense (not future tense), saying how grateful you are for having done _____ and for having _____ in your life. List how the accomplishments you have done, the things and people you have in your life, how you are feeling, and the mindset you are coming from. Write it as if these things have already come to pass.

After you write those letters to yourself, seal them and write the date you want to open them. Keep them in a safe place (but not the safe place that you forget about where they are at). Keep those letters in mind and begin to implement your gifts and talents, daily habits, tasks, goals and actions that will move you towards what is within those letters. And remember that the beauty is within the journey of what will get you towards what is written within those pages.

Another beautiful thing is now you are aware, you have grown in your consciousness of what your life can become, who you desire to grow into and how you can choose to move towards it. You have officially been commissioned.

**Chosen.**

**Anointed.**

## *Called.*

You now know some tools and resources to get you started and to use along the way. You now have a tribe and a mentor that believes in you and the potential that is inside of you, just waiting to be ignited.

You cannot play small.
You cannot stay dimmed.
Regardless of what anyone else may say.
Regardless of what the chattering voices within you may tell you.

***The world needs you.***
***We need you.***
***I need you.***
***The lives of those you will impact need you.***

Yes, YOU:

- *The entrepreneur who feels alone and doesn't know what next step to take.*

- *The exhausted mom who has been at home raising babies, wants to go back to work but isn't sure if she can actually enter the workforce again.*

- *The one that is 50 pounds overweight and needs to do something drastic to get your health back on track.*

- *The one who doesn't trust your inner wisdom, listens to everyone else and in the end, you wish you would have listened to that still small voice.*

- *The dreamer who believes you were meant for more, but you keep hiding and not sharing your message with others.*

## *STOP.*

*STOP waiting for someone else to tell you what to do.*
*STOP waiting for someone else to do it for you.*
*STOP looking for yet another book, the next conference, another podcast or course before you actually take a step and move towards your dreams.*

Darling, get up. Rise up. Stand up. Brush off the dirt from yesterday. Get over it. Get on with it. You are stronger than this.

We need your strength, your light, your love, and your story. You are a piece to this puzzle we call life and it wouldn't be complete without you.

## You *must* shine.

It's up to you now, Beautiful One. Claim your beauty, your power, your light, your purpose and your story - wholeheartedly, fully, and unapologetically. Enjoy the journey and trust that it is all happening *for* you.

Learn the lessons. Embrace the pressure. Trust the divine discontentment. Find your tribe. Be unapologetic. Shine. Fail. Pivot. Do a U-turn. Align. Inspire and ignite others to shine as well. Choose to see the best in them and in yourself, have fun, have lots of dance parties, and be YOU – the one you were created to be. Remember who you are, whose you are, and why you are here. Because you are here "for such a time as this," for a special purpose, and the time is *now*.

Let's go babe. We have work to do...


*#WeAreMeantForMore*

## Chapter 12
# PS - One last thing before you go...
## Always remember:

People are often unreasonable, irrational, and self-centered.
Forgive them anyway.
If you are kind, people may accuse you of selfish ulterior motives.
Be kind anyway.
If you are successful, you'll win some unfaithful friends and some genius enemies.
Succeed anyway.
If you are honest and sincere people may deceive you.
Be honest and sincere anyway.
What you spend years creating, others could destroy overnight.
Create anyway.
If you find serenity and happiness, some may be jealous.
Be happy anyway.
The good you do today will often be forgotten.
Do good anyway.
Give the best you have, and it will never be enough.
Give your best anyway.
In the final analysis, it is between you and God.
It was never between you and them anyway.
-Mother Teresa

**#WeAreMeantForMore**
**@CharityMajors**

# References

1. http://www.healthguidance.org/entry/16417/1/Physical-Traits-That-Are-Universally-Attractive-in-Men-and-Women.html
)

2. http://innertranquility.com.au

3. (https://nobullying.com/cyber-bullying-statistics-2014/
)

4. http://coaching.gallup.com/2013/08/

# About the Author

## About Charity Majors

As a Speaker, Author, Podcaster, Entrepreneur, Mentor, and Pageant Winner, Charity Majors empowers women to align with their purpose, take bold & inspired action and implement savvy business strategy so they confidently, authentically and unapologetically shine.

Her two favorite titles are Mom to her son, Judah and Wife to her husband, Chris. Charity and her family call Boise, Idaho, their home base. You can also find them cozying up in the mountains or adventuring all around the world, exploring above and below the ocean.

Charity is available for speaking, mentorship, and has her online courses available to empower you and your tribe to own your God-given purpose.

**Visit CharityMajors.com**

www.ingramcontent.com/pod-product-compliance
Lightning Source LLC
LaVergne TN
LVHW052100090426
835512LV00036B/2855